backyard
bird quilts

P9-EDY-726

JODIE DAVIS

©2006 Jodie Davis
Published by

An Imprint of F+W Publications

700 East State Street • Iola, WI 54990-0001
715-445-2214 • 888-457-2873
www.krausebooks.com

Our toll-free number to place an order or obtain a free catalog is (800) 258-0929.

All rights reserved. No portion of this publication may be reproduced or transmitted in any form or by any means, electronic or mechanical, including photocopy, recording, or any information storage and retrieval system, without permission in writing from the publisher, except by a reviewer who may quote brief passages in a critical article or review to be printed in a magazine or newspaper, or electronically transmitted on radio, television, or the Internet.

A portion of the proceeds from the sale of this book will be donated to Project FeederWatch at the Cornell Lab of Ornithology in Ithaca, N.Y. (See Resources, page 160, for more information about Project FeederWatch.)

Library of Congress Catalog Number: 2005935065
ISBN: 978- 0-89689-178-4

Designed by Marilyn McGrane
Edited by Maria L. Turner and Sarah Herman

Printed in China

Table of Contents

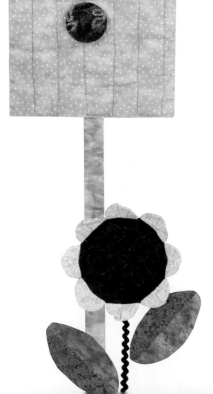

Dedication

Each winter weekend finds me scanning the back yard through the sights of binoculars and scope, tallying the numbers of birds of each species I see. Eighteen species in a day is a good count. Over time, I have learned when each bird species makes its way to and from my yard with the seasons, like clockwork. April 6, give or take a day, is the yearly debut of the hummingbirds — and I'd better have nectar out or I'll get a scolding for sure.

What's the reason for this flurry of concerted observation and record-keeping? I participate in Project FeederWatch, a Cornell Laboratory of Ornithology project that runs November through April of each year. Bird lovers all across the country participate, surveying their yards and reporting the highest number of each species they see at any given time. One can monitor her yard for 15 minutes or four hours and entering data takes just minutes online.

Thanks to all of us "citizen scientists," Cornell has used the data collected to track the migration of birds, their expanding or shrinking territories over time, and even the spread of an eye disease endemic in house finches. With the FeederWatch site constantly updated, bird lovers get a front row seat as all of this data is reported. We see the results of our efforts in learning more about the lives of birds, the impact of humans, climate, and diseases — making us as citizens, scientists!

As a small thank you for the immense joy birds give me and to support the valuable efforts of the lab, Jodie and Company will donate a portion of the royalties received from sales of this book to the FeederWatch program. What could be a more worthy cause?

Acknowledgments

I have the pleasure of working with some very talented sewers who, typical of quilters, have become my friends in the process. Thanks to Mavis Rosbach, Barb Stevenson and Joyce Woodall for your beautiful work and good cheer.

Thanks to the following companies for the wonderful products you develop and manufacture that make quilting such a pleasure and for providing materials for the projects in this book:

- Hoffman Fabrics for the luscious batik fabrics for the bedroom projects
- Mountain Mist for the wonderfully luxurious Heritage Collection of pillow forms
- Andover Fabrics Gail Kessler's Manor House for the kitchen projects
- Hobbs and its batting for every purpose
- HP for its surprisingly easy-to-use and oh-so-creative all-in-one printer
- Sulky for rayon threads in a candy box of colors
- Dritz for its ingenious WashAway foundation paper
- YLI for bird-friendly variegated quilting threads
- Down Factory for the exquisite bed pillows
- RJR Fabrics for the fabrics for the porch projects
- Coats and Clark for great piecing threads and more
- The Warm Company for Steam-a-Seam 2, which makes appliqué a breeze
- The Electric Quilt Company for its Printables line of products, including paper for foundation piecing
- American & Efird for its Mettler thread for satin stitching
- Bill Fonti, owner of Furniture & Appliance Mart, for giving us a site for our photography

Introduction

Quilters have a lot of things in common. One is a love of birds, which I found out several years ago when I started a backyard bird block-of-the-month on my Web site. Quilters responded with enthusiasm and I soon received photos of some lovely quilts made using the blocks. The reception was so great that I decided to turn the blocks into a book and asked the publisher to leave room for a gallery of quilts to showcase the talent of the online bird-loving quilters.

While the birds were on my site, I was often asked for guidance in choosing fabrics. In book format, it is easier for readers to look at the block and the shading in the patterns for help, but, as I recommended to inquiring online quilters then, I recommend to readers now to consult a bird guide when choosing your fabrics. But I suggest not getting too hung up on it. Mother Nature doesn't follow strict rules, and fabrics are very forgiving. Add that to the many reasons we love fabric!

When sitting at the computer writing paper-piecing materials lists, my fingers invariably freeze when it comes to typing in yardages. In my classes, I find there are two camps: people who economize on fabric using every last scrap and people who feel it is their job to keep fabric shops in business. With that in mind, fingers to keys, I make my best guess as to what others will use, aiming to be sure that everyone has enough fabric to complete the project. Whichever camp your tent is pitched in, please understand that the fabric amounts listed may not correspond exactly with what you use. Paper-piecing is accurate for sure, but fabric mileage varies from quilter to quilter.

Oops! It's late afternoon, time to fill the mealworm feeders again. I am the pied piper this time of year as I make my rounds, with Carolina wrens, chickadees and brown-headed nuthatches anything but bashful as they grab a worm for their chicks in my wake. My reward is their song I'm hearing now, and my reward for writing this book will be seeing the quilts you make using the patterns. Happy paper-piecing!

The Basics

Before you begin with paper-piecing the blocks for the projects in this book, take some time to review this chapter. Whether a novice or a lifelong quilter, the information covered on these pages can only help in your quest to create beautiful birds.

Tools

All that is required for these projects is a sewing machine and basic sewing tools. You will find a ¼" foot helpful for sewing the blocks together when completed, but for paper-piecing, an open-toe foot will allow you to see the lines as you sew along them.

You will need sewing shears and paper scissors, pins, a rotary mat and ruler, an iron and ironing board, and a seam ripper for those inevitable mistakes. You also may find a glue stick useful.

Choose your thread according to the fabrics selected. Gray is a good choice for most fabrics, while a light beige or even a white may work best for light fabrics. And of course, 100 percent cotton is a best bet when working with all-cotton fabrics.

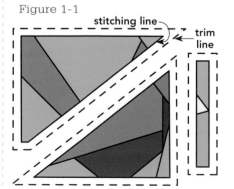

Paper-Piecing

Selecting a Foundation Material

The first step in paper-piecing is to transfer the patterns from the book to paper. The paper provides sewing lines for extremely accurate piecing, acts as a stabilizer so you needn't be concerned with grain line, and makes patching of the finished blocks easy.

Because I go through a lot of paper while designing, I keep inexpensive newsprint in my ink jet printer. But newsprint is far from an ideal paper-piecing foundation. Manufacturers have developed foundation sheets to address the needs of paper-piecers. Some are translucent, so we can see through them to better place our fabrics. There is even a water-soluble type, which totally eliminates the step of tearing out paper! I have listed some of these products in the Resources section, page 160, so you can try them.

Defining the Pattern Markings

The patterns for the blocks in this book are full size with ¼" seam allowances added. As you look at each pattern, you will notice several things.

First: Each section of the pattern is numbered. The numbers indicate the sewing sequence for the fabric pieces.

Second: Each pattern has dashed and solid lines. Dashed lines represent cutting lines and solid lines represent sewing lines.

Take a look at the pattern (Figure 1-1). The outermost line—the dashed one—is the outside edge of the block along which you will trim your block after you paper-piece it. The solid lines ¼" inside the dashed lines—a square in this case—are your sewing lines for stitching the blocks together. The other lines are the design lines along which you will sew to paper-piece.

Finally, you may notice that some patterns are the mirror image of the block you see in the photo. This is because the blocks are sewn from the marked side of the paper foundation, which is the wrong side of the finished block. For symmetrical blocks, the patterns and finished blocks look the same, but for asymmetrical blocks, the finished blocks are mirror images of the patterns.

Figure 1-1

stitching line

trim line

How to Paper-Piece

1 Make the pattern. Either trace the pattern from the book or use a copy machine to make a copy. If photocopying, make sure the images are not distorted during the process. When making your copies, be sure the page is flat to ensure accuracy in pattern sizes.

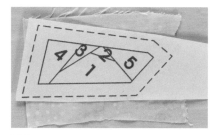

Figure 1-2

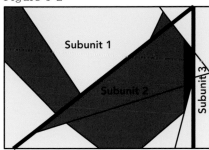

2 Remove extraneous paper by cutting away the blank paper outside the dashed lines.

Note: The areas of the block are numbered (Figure 1-2). You will be adding fabric to the block, starting with patch 1, sewing on patch 2, then adding patch 3 and so on.

3 Rough-cut a piece of fabric for subunit 1 larger than the patch itself by at least ½" all the way around. Lay the piece of fabric cut for patch 1 on the unprinted side of the paper pattern so it covers the area of patch 1, wrong side of fabric toward the plain side of the paper. Remember, the plain side of the paper is the right side of the block.

Tips

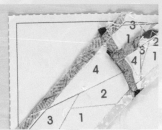

For step 2 ❯❯ To get into a paper-piecing mindset, note that the printed side of your pattern will be the wrong side of the finished block. You will be sewing with the printed side of the block facing up so you can see the lines. Your fabric will be underneath the paper, on the right side of the block. See what I mean about setting your sewing assumptions aside?

For step 3 ❯❯ Cut the fabric for your patches larger than you think they need to be. Once you develop an eye for how much you need, you can be more economical with your fabric. Especially when learning, it is better to waste fabric than have to resort to the dreaded seam ripper.

Place a pin through the fabric and paper or simply use a dab of fabric glue to hold it in place.

4 Cut a piece of fabric for patch 2 generously larger than the area of the patch itself. Place the fabric so its right side faces the fabric for patch 1, with about ¼" or more of the fabric extending into the area of patch 2.

Note: Notice that you have placed the two fabrics right sides together. All that is different from any other kind of piecing is that you have a piece of paper on top of the two fabric pieces and will be sewing on a line on the paper.

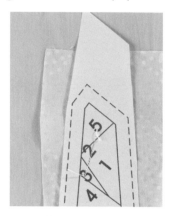 

5 Shorten the stitch length to 15 or 1.5 stitches per inch, depending on your brand of sewing machine. Place the block under the presser foot of the sewing machine, positioning it so you will start stitching in the seam allowance three or four stitches. Sew along the solid line and into the opposite seam allowance, again extending three stitches or so into the seam allowance space.

7 Fold the patch 2 fabric piece over the seam and press it in place.

Tip

A shortened stitch length in step 5 will make your job of removing the paper from your blocks easier, thanks to the perforations added by the needle going into the paper more often.

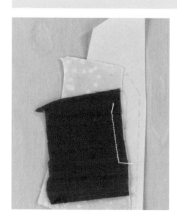

6 Flip up patch 2 to be sure it covers the area marked 2 in the pattern when it is pressed into place, as shown at left. Trim the seam allowance to ¼", using a scissors so you are sure not to cut through the paper.

Things to Remember

1. You are always sewing with fabrics right sides together.

2. When you are ready to sew and have the block under the foot of your sewing machine, the lower patch number (the one you just sewed) will be to your left, and the patch you are adding will be to your right. The bulk of the fabric—that you will fold back to cover the space on the paper—will be extending to your left. Go ahead and sew a block with this in mind. It will help you to keep from sitting and scratching your head, trying to go through the steps mentally again. It makes the process automatic—and results correct.

8A Lay the fabric for patch 3 face up on the sewing machine bed and place the block on top.

8B I have flipped it here to show you what it looks like from underneath, but remember: sew from the paper side (the marked side of the block). Stitch in the marked line between the areas marked 2 and 3.

11 Lay the subunit, fabric side down (marked paper side up), on a cutting mat and use a rotary cutter and ruler to trim the edges of the subunit piece along the dashed lines. This leaves a ¼" seam allowance. Make sure you cut through the paper foundation and fabric.

Note: Leave the paper foundation in place until after the quilt top is completed. Subunits and blocks are easier to align this way and will not become distorted by the tearing process. Also, do not worry about the grain line of the fabrics in your block. One of the beauties of foundation piecing is that the foundation stabilizes the fabrics, and as a result, it is unnecessary to follow grain-line rules strictly when cutting fabric.

9 Press, trim the seam allowances and press patch 3 into place, as shown in the sequential photos above.

10 Finish paper-piecing all the patches, pressing each subunit along the way.

Tips

For step 8 ›› While paper-piecing, I use a mini-fluorescent light from a hardware store turned on so I can see the fabric underneath the block from the printed side of the paper. It sure helps with placement!

For step 9 ›› Use a press cloth when pressing on the printed side of the pattern, as the printer ink may otherwise transfer to your iron.

Paper-Piecing Curves

This is so easy I don't know why someone else didn't think of it. The extra fabric created by sewing on the curve is folded into small pleats. The Hummingbird Block on page 125 is the only one that uses curved pieces.

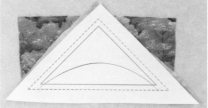 

1 Paper-piece as usual, stitching on the curved line, as shown above.

2 Trim.

3 When you fold the subunit 2 fabric back, make pleats, as shown in the sequential photos above, to take up the extra fabric created by the curve.

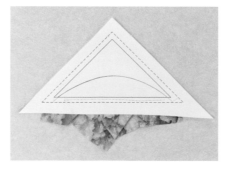 

4 Pin and baste the pleats, as shown in the sequential photos above.

5 Trim along the dashed lines

Subunits

Some block designs require two or more paper-pieced sections to complete them. Due to the design lines, it can't be sewn in one piece. And so, when I design the block, I divide it into one or more sections and call these "subunits." These are then sewn together into a complete block. Note also that the sections are joined by angled seams—and I'll show you a trick that makes sewing them together foolproof.

To match the subunits:

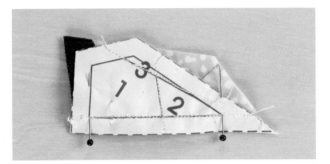

1 Hold them together, right sides together, with their straight raw edges matching.

2 Push a straight pin vertically down into the left-hand corner of the stitching lines on the top subunit.

3 Push the pin vertically straight down into the matching corner of the stitching lines on the other subunit. Do the same for the right side.

4 Pin the two subunits together, as shown above.

5 Remove the pins at the corners.

6 Sew along the stitching line.

7 Remove the paper from the seam allowances and press.

Tip

>> Color-code or mark your patterns so you stitch the correct fabric in the proper place in your block. When making multiple blocks, I make an extra copy of the pattern, color-code it and use it as a key so I can easily see where the different fabrics go. You can also mark your actual paper foundations. For instance, put a "B" for brown fabric in the appropriate areas and an "F" for the flowered background in those areas.

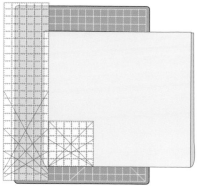

Figure 1-3

Figure 1-4

Figure 1-5

Rotary Cutting

For the projects in this book, you will need a cutting mat, rotary cutter and rotary cutting rulers, which are among the basics needed for quilting. Try a 6" x 24" clear rotary cutting ruler and a 10½" or larger square ruler.

The object in rotary cutting is to make straight, even cuts as close to the fabric grain as possible. This way squares and rectangles are cut on the lengthwise and crosswise grain, assuring that they will not distort as they would if cut with bias edges. Note that when paper-piecing, however, the paper acts as a stabilizer, so you need not be concerned with grain line when cutting any of the paper-pieced fabric pieces.

Note: The illustrations are for right-handed quilters. If you are left-handed, simply do everything in reverse.

1 On the cutting mat, fold the fabric in half lengthwise, matching the selvedge edges, with the raw edges to your right and left and the fold closest to you.

2 Place the square ruler along the folded edge, making sure it is aligned with the fold.

3 Place the 6" x 24" ruler next to the square ruler, butting the edges and having the long ruler cover the uneven raw edges of the fabric (Figure 1-3).

4 Remove the square ruler and make a clean cut along the edges of the longer ruler (Figure 1-4).

Cutting Strips

1 Align the just clean-cut edge of the fabric with the desired marking on the ruler.

2 Cut (Figure 1-5).

Cutting Squares

1 For example, to finish 4", cut a strip 4½" (the ½" allows for ¼" seam allowances).

2 Crosscut the strip into 4½" squares (Figure 1-6).

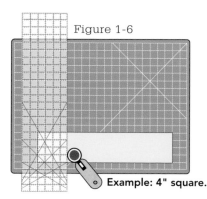

Figure 1-6

Example: 4" square.

Tip

Always roll the cutter away from you. For a crisp cut, use even pressure and start rolling before you reach the fabric and continue after it. You may need to stop cutting halfway through to reposition your hand on the ruler. Also, get in the habit of closing your cutter before putting it down or purchase one with a self-retracting blade.

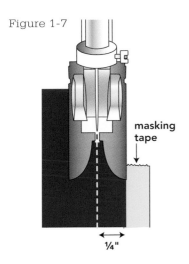

Figure 1-7

Making Seam Allowances

For accurate piecing, it is paramount that you sew an accurate ¼" seam allowance.

Many sewing machines come equipped with a presser foot that measures ¼" from the stitching line to the right edge of the foot.

1 Test your machine by sewing a sample and measuring the seam allowance.

2 If it is not ¼", place a piece of masking tape on your machine to mark the ¼" seam allowance (Figure 1-7).

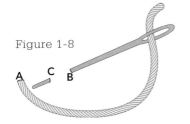

Figure 1-8

Embroidery

Simple embroidery is used sparingly in this book, both by hand and by machine. Embroidered projects use several stitches that are easy for the beginner to master. My favorite embroidery floss is made by DMC® and is widely available at crafts and sewing stores. For machine embroidery, I use many threads, including Mettler and Sulky.

Figure 1-9

Stem Stitch

1 Come up at A, the beginning of the line of stitching (Figure 1-8).

2 Go in at B and bring the needle up at C along the line of stitching (Figure 1-8).

3 Continue working this way, making each new stitch the same length as the previous one (D and E) and keeping the stitches even and longer than the spaces between them (Figure 1-9).

Chain Stitch

1 Come up at A (Figure 1-11).

2 Hold the thread down with your thumb, go down at B (as close as possible to A) and come back up at C with the needle tip over the thread (Figure 1-11).

3 Repeat along the marked line, forming a chain (Figure 1-12).

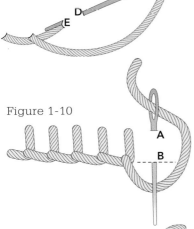

Figure 1-10

Figure 1-11

Buttonhole Stitch

Go in at A and out at B, with the thread to the back of the needle, making even stitches (Figure 1-10).

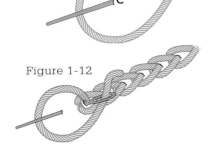

Figure 1-12

Tip

Your thread will often twist from constant needle action. To remedy this, drop the needle and let it dangle freely until the thread unwinds.

Assembly and Finishing

Layering the Quilt

Before you quilt your piece, you must assemble the three layers—top, batting and backing—and secure them to prevent slipping during quilting.

1 Press the quilt top and the backing.

2 Lay the backing on the work surface and smooth it. Use masking tape to secure the edges.

3 Place the batting on top of the backing, smoothing it in place.

4 Lay the quilt top, right-side up, on top of the batting.

5 Secure the layers together by either basting them or safety pinning (Figure 1-13). The stitches or pins should be 4" to 6" apart.

Machine Quilting

To quilt straight lines of quilting by machine, use a walking foot. A walking foot helps to feed the layers of the quilt evenly, thereby preventing puckers. As an added benefit, your stitches will be even.

For free-motion work (outline quilting, stippling swirls or meandering around areas), use a darning foot and lower the feed dogs of the sewing machine. This requires practice.

To learn more about quilting, invest in one or more books on the subject and check with your local quilt shop to take a class. Several great books on the subject can be found through KP Books (Resources, page 160).

Adding a Hanging Sleeve

1 Cut a strip of fabric 6" to 8" wide and 1" to 2" shorter than the width of the quilt at the top edge.

2 Hem the short ends by pressing under ¼" twice and topstitching (Figure 1-14).

3 Fold the fabric strip in half lengthwise, wrong sides together.

4 Seam the long raw edges together, using a ¼" seam allowance.

5 Fold the tube so that the seam is centered on one side (to be the back, against the quilt backing) and press the seam allowances open.

6 Pin the tube to the back of the quilt.

7 Stitch the binding to the quilt (Figure 1-15), as instructed in the Binding section that follows.

Figure 1-13

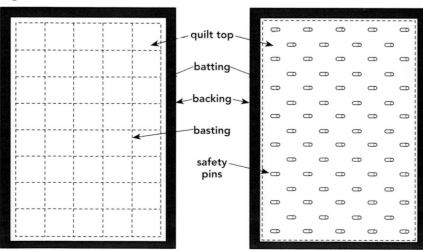

quilt top
batting
backing
basting
safety pins

Figure 1-14

½"

Figure 1-15

Figure 1-16

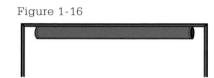

Figure 1-17

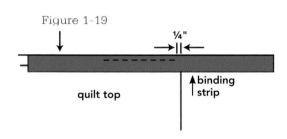

Figure 1-18

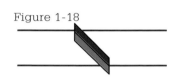

Figure 1-19

¼"

quilt top

binding strip

Figure 1-20

quilt top

Figure 1-21

fold

quilt top

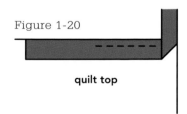

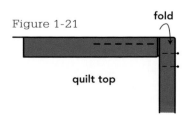

8 Continue with sleeve before hand-sewing the binding.

9 Push the tube up so the top edge covers about half of the binding, pin and sew the bottom edge of the sleeve to the quilt backing (Figure 1-16). This will provide some "give" to accommodate the hanging rod.

To hang the quilt, insert a curtain rod or wooden dowel into the sleeve and suspend the quilt on brackets. Or attach screw eyes or drill holes in the ends of a length of lathe and slip the eyes or holes over small nails in the wall.

Binding

1 Cut fabric into 2½"-wide bias strips.

2 Stitch the binding strips together on the diagonal, end to end to form a continuous strip (Figure 1-17).

3 Trim and press seams open (Figure 1-18) and then press binding in half lengthwise so wrong sides are facing.

4 Trim batting and backing even with the quilt top.

5 Place the binding strip along one edge of the right side of the quilt top, matching raw edges.

6 Leave the first 4" or so of the binding free and stitch the binding to the quilt, using a ¼" seam allowance. Stop stitching ¼" from the corner (Figure 1-19). Backstitch and remove the quilt from the machine.

7 Turn the quilt to prepare for sewing the next edge and fold the binding up, creating a 45-degree angle fold (Figure 1-20).

8 Fold the binding down (Figure 1-21), having the fold even with the top edge of the quilt and the raw edge aligned with the side of the quilt.

9 Begin at the edge and stitch the binding to the quilt, stopping ¼" from the next corner. Backstitch and remove the quilt from the machine.

Figure 1-22

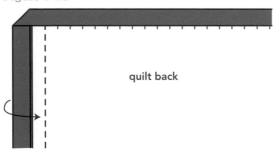

Figure 1-23

quilt back

Figure 1-24

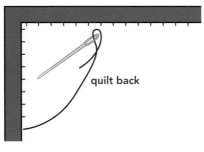

quilt back

10 Continue the folding and stitching process for the remaining corners.

11 Stop stitching when you are within approximately 4" of the starting point.

12 Cut the binding end so it overlaps the unstitched binding at the beginning by at about 2".

13 Cut the end diagonally.

14 Turn the diagonal edge under ¼" and insert the beginning end inside the fold (Figure 1-22). Finish sewing the binding to the quilt.

15 Fold the binding to the back of the quilt over the raw edges of the quilt "sandwich," covering the machine stitching (Figure 1-23). A miter will appear on the front.

16 Whipstitch the binding to the back of the quilt (Figure 1-24).

Summer Porch Projects

Today, so many people think of their porches as another room in
their home, complete with lavish furniture. The projects in this
chapter help you give a personal touch to your porch—or sunroom
or gazebo—and add even more birds to the great outdoors!

Placemats

Finished size: 11" x 17"
Made by: Barb Stevenson

Materials
(for four placemats)

See the small size simple cardinal and simple bluebird blocks on pages 150 and 153 for fabric requirements, or select different birds of choice.

» ¼-yard flower print fabric (placemat top)

» 1½ yards striped fabric (placemat top and backing)

» ¼-yard red fabric (cardinal block insert border strips and binding)

» ¼-yard blue fabric (bluebird block insert border strips and binding)

» ¾-yard batting

» Coordinating thread

Cutting Plan
(for each placemat)

From the flower print, cut:
  • one 1½" x 5½" piece
  • one 5½" x 7" piece
From the striped fabric, cut:
  • one 11½" x 12½" panel (with the stripe runnning lengthwise)
From the red fabric, cut:
  • two 1" x 42" insert border strips
  • two 2¼" x 42" binding strips
From the blue fabric, cut:
  • two 1" x 42" insert border strips
  • two 2¼" x 42" binding strips
From the backing, cut:
  • four 12½" x 18½" pieces
From the batting, cut:
  • four 12½" x 18½" pieces

»»To whet your appetite for paper-piecing birds, I offer these simplified patterns: a cardinal and a bluebird. With fewer pattern pieces than the larger birds, they work up quickly and are just right for the small scale required of this project.««

Instructions

Note: All seam allowances are ¼" unless otherwise instructed.

Step 1

Figure 2-1

Figure 2-2

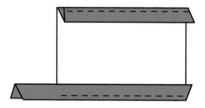

Figure 2-3

Figure 2-4

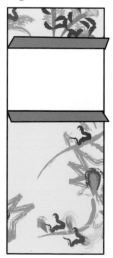
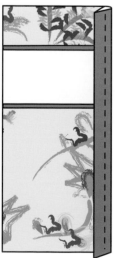

Assemble the Placemat Top

Refer to the layout diagrams on the next page, if necessary, while assembling the placemat tops.

1. Paper-piece the bird blocks, following the instructions on pages 9 through 13, 150 and 153.

2. Press the 1"-wide insert border strip in half lengthwise (Figure 2-1). With raw edges even, baste the strip to the top edge of the bird block.

3. Trim the insert strip even with the side edges of the block (Figure 2-2).

4. Repeat steps 2 and 3 for the bottom edge of the block.

5. Stitch the smaller flowered piece to the top edge of the block and the larger flowered fabric piece to the bottom edge of the block. Press the seam allowances toward the block and press the insert strips away from the block (Figure 2-3).

6. Matching raw edges, baste an insert strip to the right edge of the bird block-flower fabric assembly.

7. Lay the striped piece on top, matching raw edges, and stitch in place (Figure 2-4). Press the insert strip toward the striped fabric.

8. Remove the paper from the bird block.

9. Hand stitch buttons or beads for the bird eyes.

1" x 5"

3½" x 5"

11" x 12"

5" x 6½"

Cardinal Placemat Layout Diagram

Finish the Placemat

1. Layer the placemat and trim the batting and backing fabric to match the size of the pieced placemat top.

2. Bind and quilt the placemat, as instructed on pages 16 through 18.

3. Press.

1" x 5"

3½" x 5"

11" x 12"

5" x 6½"

Bluebird Placemat Layout Diagram

Napkins

Finished size: 16" square
Made by: Jodie Davis

Materials

(for set of four napkins)

» 1 yard fabric (or ½-yard each of two coordinating fabrics, as shown in the photo)

» Coordinating thread

Cutting Plan

From the fabric, cut:
- four 16½" squares

Instructions

Note: All seam allowances are ¼" unless otherwise instructed.

1. Press ¼" to the wrong side along each napkin edge. Repeat.

2. Topstitch a scant ¼" from the folded edge.

3. Press.

»»While purchasing fabric for your placemats, buy extra and make coordinating napkins in a snap.««

Flag Sign

Finished size: 14" x 24"
Made by: Jodie Davis

Materials
(for four placemats)

See the robin bird block on page 112 for fabric requirements, or select a different bird of choice.

» 1⅛ yards striped fabric (flag stripes and backing)

» ⅜-yard red fabric (flag stripes)

» ¼-yard blue fabric (binding)

» 20" x 30" piece batting

» Coordinating thread

» Embroidery thread*

» Stabilizer*

» Temporary spray adhesive*

» 5 hanks pearl cotton thread*

» Cardboard

» Lettering template (page 29)

*Used in this project: Sulky 40 rayon #2105; Sulky Tear Easy Stabilizer; 505 Spray and Fix; and DMC Pearl Cotton.

Cutting Plan
(for each placemat)

From the striped fabric, cut:
- two 2½" x 16½" strips
- two 2½" x 24½" strips

From the red fabric, cut:
- two 2½" x 16½" strips
- one 2½" x 24½" strips

From the blue fabric, cut:
- two 2¼" x 42" binding strips

»»The harbinger of spring proclaims his industriousness in this perky wallhanging. The tassel is easy to make out of fabulous threads.««

Instructions

Note: All seam allowances are ¼" unless otherwise instructed.

Step 1

Figure 2-5

strips are 2½" x 16½" cut size

Figure 2-6

strips are 2½" x 16½" cut size

Figure 2-7

Figure 2-8

Assemble the Flag Top

Refer to the layout diagram on the next page, if necessary, while assembling the flag top.

1. Paper-piece the bird block, following the instructions on pages 9 through 13 and 112.

2. Stitch the 16½"-long strips together, alternating the fabrics—stripe, red, stripe, red—to form the right side of the flag (Figure 2-5). Press the seam allowances to one side.

3. Stitch the 24½"-long strips together—stripe, red, stripe — to form the bottom of the flag (Figure 2-6). Press the seam allowances to one side.

4. Trace the full-size lettering from the next page and transfer it to the red strips.

5. Cut a piece of stabilizer large enough to cover the back of the embroidered area and secure it to the area with spray adhesive.

6. Embroider the letters either by hand or machine, referring to page 15 for handwork, if necessary. The sample here was satin-stitched by machine.

7. Remove the stabilizer and press.

8. Stitch the robin block, with right sides together, to the left side of the shorter section of strips (Figure 2-7). Press the seam allowance to one side.

9. Stitch the longer set of strips with right sides together to the bottom of the robin block (Figure 2-8). Press the seam allowances to one side.

10. Remove the paper from the bird block.

11. Hand stitch buttons or beads for the bird eyes and embroider the legs, if desired.

Finish the Flag

1. Layer and bind the flag, following the instructions on pages 16 through 18.

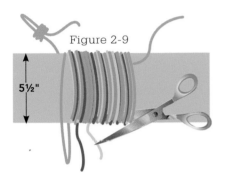

Figure 2-9

5½"

2. Cut a piece of cardboard 5½" wide.

3. Wind the pearl cotton onto the cardboard, having the trailing ends at the bottom (Figure 2-9).

Figure 2-10

4. Thread a needle with a length of the pearl cotton, run it under the threads at the top edge of the cardboard and tie in a secure knot, leaving long ends to attach the tassel to the quilt.

5. Cut the threads at the bottom edge of the cardboard and remove the cardboard.

6. Arrange the threads neatly in place and tie the tassel together with a piece of pearl cotton about ¾" from the top (Figure 2-10). Trim the bottom of the tassel neatly.

7. Hand stitch the tassel to the top left corner of the flag.

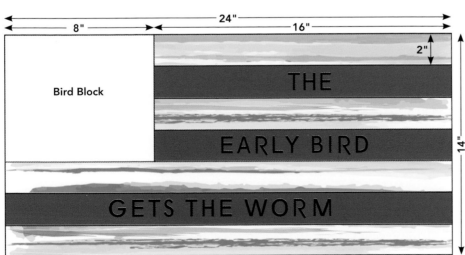

Flag Layout Diagram

24"

8" 16"

2"

Bird Block

14"

THE

EARLY BIRD

GETS THE WORM

THE EARLY BIRD GETS THE WORM

Lettering Template

Porch Pillows

These two pillows are perfect for brightening a garden bench or chair.

Mock Corded Pillow

Materials

(for four placemats)

See the robin bird block on page 112 for fabric requirements, or select a different bird of choice.

» ½-yard flower print fabric (borders and backing)

» ⅛ -yard blue fabric (insert border strips)

» 2 yards 1"-wide cording

» 14" square pillow form

» Coordinating thread

Cutting Plan

(for each placemat)

From the flower print, cut:
- two 3½" x 8½" side border strips
- two 3½" x 14½" top and bottom border strips
- two 10½" x 14½" backing pieces

From the blue fabric, cut:
- one 1" x 42" insert border strip

»»The lovely wide-corded edge on the Mock Corded Pillow can be a bit of a challenge for beginners, but is well worth it for the more advanced sewer.««

Finished size: 14" square
Made by: Barb Stevenson

Instructions

Note: All seam allowances are ¼" unless otherwise instructed.

Step 1

Figure 2-11

Assemble the Pillow Top

Refer to the layout diagram on the next page, if necessary, while assembling the pillow top.

1. Paper-piece the bird block, following the instructions on pages 9 through 13 and 112.

2. Press the 1"-wide blue insert border strip in half lengthwise (Figure 2-11). With raw edges even, baste the strip to the top edge of the bird block.

3. Trim the insert strip even with the side edges of the block (Figure 2-12).

4. Repeat steps 2 and 3 for the bottom edge of the block and then for the sides.

5. With right sides together, stitch the 3½" x 8½" side border strips to the sides of the bird block (Figure 2-13). Press the seam allowances toward the flower print fabric.

6. Stitch the 3½" x 14½" top and bottom border strips to the top and bottom of the pillow top (Figure 2-14). Press the seam allowances toward the flower print fabric.

7. Press under ¼" on one long edge of each pillow backing piece. Press under another 1". Topstitch the hem in place.

8. Remove the paper from the bird block.

9. Hand stitch buttons or beads for the bird eyes and embroider the legs, if desired.

Figure 2-12

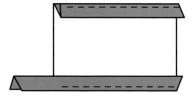

Figure 2-13

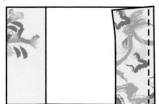

Figure 2-14

Figure 2-15

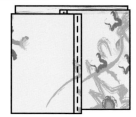

Finish the Pillow

1. Lay the pillow top right-side up.

2. Place the pillow back on top of the pillow top with right sides down, aligning the raw edges and overlapping the hemmed edges (Figure 2-15). Pin, avoiding pin placement near the corners.

3. Align the straight edges of the Corner Cutting Template on one corner of the assembled pillow (Figure 2-16) and trim the pillow top, as shown, using a rotary cutter, or mark and trim with scissors. Repeat for the three remaining corners.

4. Stitch ¼" from the edges all the way around the pillow.

5. Turn right-side out and press.

6. Place the cording inside the pillow and push up against the outer edge as close as possible to the outer seam. Trim the cording so the ends just meet.

7. Use a zipper foot and work from the right side of the pillow to stitch close to the cording, crowding it close to the outer edge. Leave about 4" open.

8. Pull the cording 4" at each end to gather the fabric at the corners of the pillow. Cut so the cord ends butt. Tack the ends together. Push them back into place and finish the topstitching.

9. Insert the pillow form.

Figure 2-16

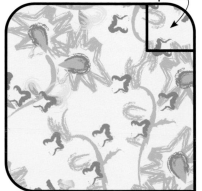

Corner Cutting Template

Mock Corded Pillow Layout Diagram

Bird Block with Insert Border

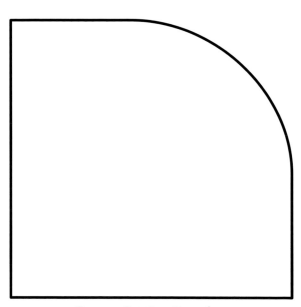

Corner Cutting Template

Knife-Edge Pillow

Materials

See the chickadee bird block on page 146 for fabric requirements, or select a different bird of choice.

» ½-yard flower print fabric (borders and backing)

» ⅛-yard red fabric (insert border strips)

» 16" square pillow form

» Coordinating thread

Cutting Plan
(for each placemat)

From the flower print, cut:

- two 4½" x 8½" side border pieces
- two 4½" x 16½" top and bottom border pieces
- two 9½" x 12½" pieces for the pillow backing
- two 2½" x 12½" backing side pieces
- two 2½" x 16½" backing top and bottom pieces

From the red fabric, cut:

- one 1" x 42" insert border strip

»»Choose any bird you like for the easy Knife-Edge

Pillow to enjoy all summer long.««

Finished size: 16" square
Made by: Barb Stevenson

Instructions

Note: All seam allowances are ¼" unless otherwise instructed.

Assemble the Pillow Top

Refer to the layout diagram on page 36, if necessary, while assembling the pillow top.

1. Paper-piece the bird block, following the instructions on pages 9 through 13 and 146.

2. Press the 1"-wide red insert border strip in half lengthwise (Figure 2-17). With raw edges even, baste the strip to the top edge of the bird block.

3. Trim the insert strip even with the side edges of the block (Figure 2-18).

4. Repeat steps 2 and 3 for the bottom edge of the block and then for the sides.

5. With right sides together, stitch the side border pieces to the sides of the bird block (Figure 2-19). Press seam allowances toward the flowered fabrics.

6. Stitch the top and bottom border pieces to the top and bottom of the block assembly (Figure 2-20). Press the seam allowances toward the flowered fabrics.

7. Remove the paper from the bird block.

8. Hand stitch buttons or beads for the bird eyes and embroider the legs, if desired.

Step 1

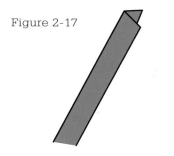

Figure 2-17

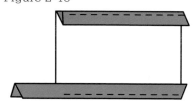

Figure 2-18

Figure 2-19

Figure 2-20

Figure 2-21

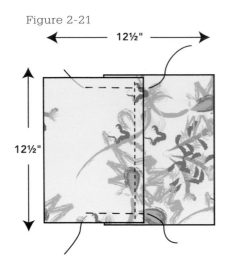

← 12½" →

12½"

Assemble the Pillow Back

1. Press under ¼" on one long edge of each 9½" x 12½" pillow backing piece. Press under another 1". Topstitch the hem in place.

2. Overlap the finished edges of the pillow back pieces, with right sides up, so they form a 12½" square. Pin and baste the overlapping edges together (Figure 2-21).

3. Stitch a 2½" x 12½" backing side piece with right sides together to each side of the backing (Figure 2-22). Press seam allowances to the outside.

4. Stitch a 2½" x 16½" backing top and bottom piece with right sides together to the top and bottom of the backing assembly (Figure 2-23). Press the seam allowances to the outside.

Finish the Pillow

1. Pin the pillow front and back with right sides together, matching raw edges.

2. Stitch ¼" from the edges all the way around the pillow, overlapping the beginning and ends of the stitching.

3. Turn right-side out and press.

4. Mark a line 2" in from the raw edge of the pillow front and topstitch along the line (Figure 2-24).

5. Insert the pillow form.

Figure 2-22

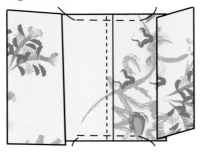

Figure 2-23

Figure 2-24

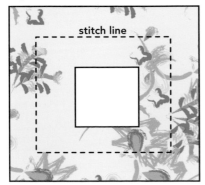

stitch line

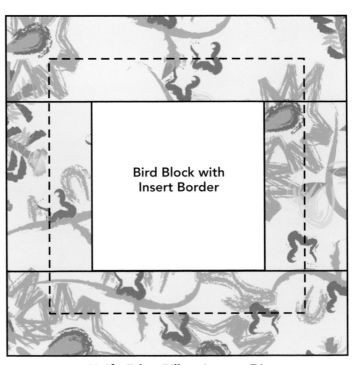

Bird Block with Insert Border

Knife-Edge Pillow Layout Diagram

Kitchen Projects

Our kitchen/dining area looks out over our backyard pond and garden, which is filled with every imaginable type of bird feeder. A scope on a tripod brings us so close to the birds that I can see a hummingbird's tongue as he preens clear across the yard. Gail Kessler's Manor House fabric line from Andover Fabrics proved perfect for my kitchen/dining area. This is an ongoing line, so the designs will change over time, but you will find it has the same look so you can achieve close to the same results shown in the projects.

Table Runner

Finished size: 12" x 28"
Made by: Joyce Woodall

Materials

See the robin and towhee bird blocks on pages 112 and 118 for fabric requirements, or select different birds of choice.

» ½-yard flower print fabric (center square and border strips)

» ½-yard striped fabric (backing)

» ⅛-yard red fabric (insert border strips)

» ⅛-yard each of four fabrics (prairie points)

» 12½" x 28½" piece batting

Cutting Plan

From the flower print, cut:
- one 8½" square center piece
- two 2½" x 24½" side border strips
- two 2½" x 12½" top and bottom border strips

From the striped fabric, cut:
- one 12½" x 28½" backing piece

From the red fabric, cut:
- two 1" x 42" insert border strips

From each of the four fabrics for the prairie points, cut:
- nine 2½" squares for prairie points (you will have a few extra)

»» A pair of backyard birds adorns this table runner, setting the stage for a winner of a centerpiece. The prairie points are simple folded squares basted to the edge of the runner before it is turned. ««

Instructions

Note: All seam allowances are ¼" unless otherwise instructed.

Assemble the Table Runner Top

Refer to the layout diagram on the next page while assembling the table runner top.

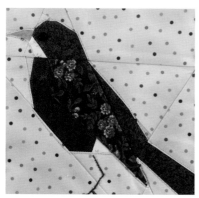 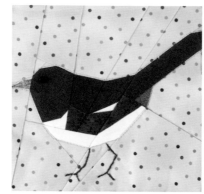

Step 1: Use two different bird blocks to grace each end of the table runner, or choose just one type of block and make it twice to be repeated on each end.

1. Paper-piece the two bird blocks following the instructions on pages 9 through 13, 112 and 118.

2. Press one 1"-wide red insert border strip in half lengthwise (Figure 3-1).

3. With raw edges even, baste the strip to one side edge of the bird block (Figure 3-2).

4. Trim the insert strip even with the top and bottom edges of the block (Figure 3-3). Repeat for the three remaining edges of the block.

5. Repeat steps 2 through 4 for the remaining bird block.

6. With right sides together, stitch the 8½" square to the top of one block (Figure 3-4), then the other (Figure 3-5), connecting the two. Press the seam allowances toward the square.

7. With right sides together, stitch the side border strips to the long edges of the runner (Figure 3-6). Press seam allowances toward the border pieces.

8. With right sides together, stitch the top and bottom border pieces to the short edges of the runner (Figure 3-7). Press the seam allowances toward the border.

9. Remove the paper from the bird blocks.

Figure 3-1

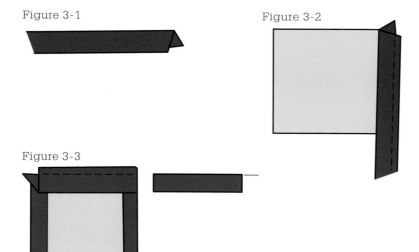

Figure 3-2

Figure 3-3

Figure 3-5

Figure 3-4

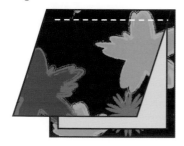 

Figure 3-6

Figure 3-7

Finish the Table Runner

1. Fold the prairie point squares in half diagonally, and in half again, as shown (Figure 3-8). Press.

2. Pin five prairie points to the short edges of the table runner top and 12 to each of the long edges. Baste in place (Figure 3-9).

3. Lay the table runner right-side up on a flat surface, lay the backing on top right-side down and then lay the batting on top of both, with raw edges of all layers matching. Pin.

4. Stitch around the edges, leaving a 6" to 8" opening in the stitching for turning. Trim across the corners.

5. Turn right-side out using a pointed object to push the corners out.

6. Whipstitch the opening closed.

7. Quilt the table runner by outlining the birds and sewing around the blocks. Add more quilting, if desired.

Figure 3-9

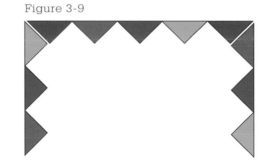

Figure 3-8

Table Runner Layout Diagram

Bird Block

Bird Block

Chair Pads

Finished size: 15" square
Made by: Joyce Woodall

Materials
(for one chair pad)

See the robin, towhee, wren and chickadee bird blocks on pages 112, 118, 121 and 146 for fabric requirements, or select different birds of choice.

» ¼-yard flowered fabric (borders)

» ¼-yard striped fabric (backing)

» ¼-yard red fabric (insert border strips and ties)

» 2 15" squares batting

» Coordinating thread

» Border top and bottom pattern (page 45)

» Border side pattern (page 46)

Cutting Plan

From the flower print, cut:
- two side border strips from pattern on page 46
- two top and bottom border strips from pattern on page 45

From the striped fabric, cut:
- one 15½" square for the backing

From the red fabric, cut:
- one 1" x 42" insert border strip
- one 3" x 42" tie strip

»»Even plain chairs become special when adorned with these bird chair pads.

I used two layers of batting in my pads since my chairs have cushioned seats.

If you have hard seats, use batting with more loft and more layers.««

Instructions

Note: All seam allowances are ¼" unless otherwise instructed.

Use different birds for each chair pad in your set, as shown here, or make all of them using the same bird block.

Figure 3-10

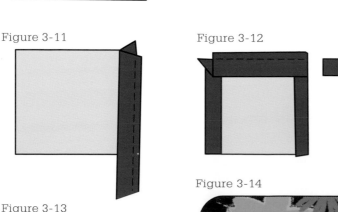

Figure 3-11

Figure 3-12

Figure 3-13

Figure 3-14

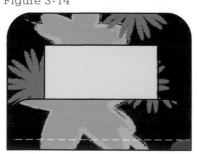

Assemble the Chair Pad Top

Refer to the layout diagram on the next page, if necessary, while assembling the chair pad top.

1. Paper-piece the bird block, following the instructions on pages 9 through 13, 112, 118, 121 and 146.

2 Press the 1"-wide red insert border strip in half lengthwise (Figure 3-10).

3. With raw edges even, baste the strip to one side edge of the bird block (Figure 3-11).

4. Trim the insert strip even with the top and bottom edges of the block (Figure 3-12).

5. Repeat steps 2 through 4 for the remaining edges of the block.

6. With right sides together, stitch the side border pieces to the side of the block (Figure 3-13). Press the seam allowances toward the center border.

7. Stitch the top and bottom border pieces to the top and bottom edges of the chair pad (Figure 3-14). Press seam allowances toward the border pieces.

8. Remove the paper from the bird block.

9. Hand stitch buttons or beads for the bird eyes and embroider the legs, if desired.

Figure 3-15

topstitch

Figure 3-16

Figure 3-17

Finish the Chair Pad

1. Fold the tie strip in half lengthwise and then fold the raw edges in to meet at the center (Figure 3-15). Topstitch close to the edge.

2. Cut the strip into four segments and baste to the back of the chair pad as shown (Figure 3-16).

3. Use the chair pad top and bottom border pattern to trim the corners of the chair pad backing corners into curves (Figure 3-17).

4. Lay the layers of batting on a flat surface and then lay the backing fabric on top right-side up, followed by the pieced chair pad right-side down. Pin the layers together.

5. Stitch around the layers, leaving a 6" opening for turning.

6. Turn chair pad right-side out, whipstitch the opening closed and press.

7. Quilt the chair pads by stitching around the birds and along the inserted binding.

Bird Block with Insert Border

Chair Pad Layout Diagram

Chair Pad Top and Bottom Border Pattern

cut 2

place on fold

Chair Pad Side Border Pattern

cut 2

Placemats

Finished size: 12" x 16"
Made by: Jodie Davis

Materials
(for one placemat)

See the cardinal, hummingbird, goldfinch and blue jay bird blocks on pages 115, 125, 131 and 140 for fabric requirements, or select different birds of choice.

» ¼-yard flower print fabric (borders)

» ⅛-yard red or green fabric (insert border strips)

» ½-yard beige fabric (bird name background and backing)

» Hand or machine embroidery thread

» 12½" x 16½" piece batting

» Lettering template (pages 50 and 51)

Cutting Plan

From the flower print, cut:
- two 2½" x 8½" side border strips
- two 2½" x 17½" top and bottom border strips

From the red or green fabric, cut:
- two 1" x 42" insert border strips

From the beige fabric, cut:
- one 6" x 8" rectangle for the bird name background panel
- one 12½" x 16½" piece for the backing

»»These placemats work up quickly using only one bird block. Add the lettering by machine as I did, or by hand if you prefer.««

Instructions

Note: All seam allowances are ¼" unless otherwise instructed.

Assemble the Placemat Top

Refer to the layout diagram on page 50, if necessary, while assembling the placemat tops.

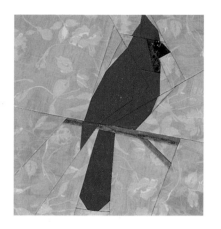

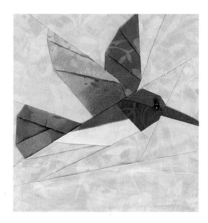

Step 1: Use four different bird blocks, as shown above, with one each on a set of four placemats, or choose just one type of bird block and make it four times for a matching set of placemats.

1. Paper-piece the bird blocks, following the instructions on pages 9 through 13, 115, 125, 131 or 140.

2. Transfer the lettering of your choice to the beige rectangle and machine satin stitch them, or turn to page 15 for hand embroidery stitch instructions.

3. Press one 1"-wide red or green insert border strip in half lengthwise (Figure 3-18).

4. With raw edges even, baste the strip to one side edge of the bird block (Figure 3-19).

5. Trim the insert strip even with the top and bottom edges of the block.

6. Repeat steps 3 through 5 for the other side of the block.

Figure 3-18

Figure 3-19

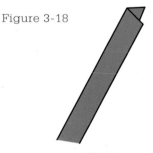
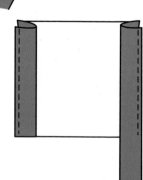

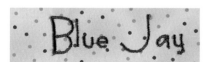
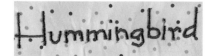

Step 2: Stitch the bird names to match the bird blocks you choose.

Figure 3-20

Figure 3-21

Figure 3-22

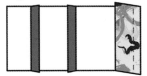

Figure 3-23

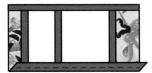

Figure 3-24

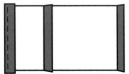

Figure 3-25

7. With right sides together, stitch the embroidered rectangle to the left side of the bird block (Figure 3-20). Press seam allowances toward the embroidered rectangle (Figure 3-21).

8. With raw edges even, baste an insert strip to the left raw edge of the embroidered rectangle (Figure 3-22).

9. With right sides together, stitch the side border strips to the sides of the placemat (Figure 3-23). Press seam allowances toward the border.

10. With raw edges even, baste an insert strip to the top and bottom edge of the placemat (Figure 3-24). Trim the insert strip even with the side edges of the Placemat.

11. With right sides together, stitch the top and bottom border strips to the top and bottom of the placemat (Figure 3-25). Press seam allowances toward the border.

12. Remove the paper from the bird blocks.

13. Hand stitch the buttons or beads for the bird eyes and hand- or machine-embroider the bird legs in place, if desired.

Finish the Placemat

1. Lay the batting on a flat surface, lay the backing on top right-side up and lay the placemat top on top of both, right-side down, with raw edges of all layers matching. Pin.

2. Stitch around the edges, leaving a 4" opening in the stitching for turning.

3. Trim across the corners.

4. Turn right-side out using a pointed object to push the corners out.

5. Whipstitch the opening closed.

6. Quilt the placemat by stitching around the bird, inside the writing and around the bird blocks.

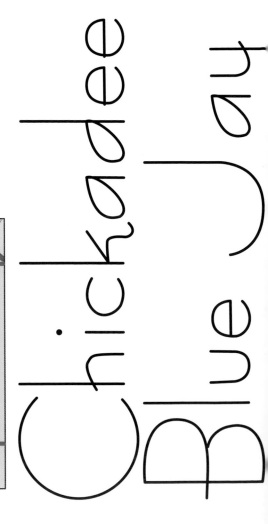

Placemat Layout Diagram

Canada Goose

Woodpecker

Goldfinch

Robin

Towhee

Bluebird

Cardinal

Hummingbird

Kingfisher

Wren

Potholder

Finished size: 8" square
Made by: Jodie Davis

Materials

(for one potholder)

See the Canada goose and woodpecker bird blocks on pages 134 and 143 for fabric requirements, or select different birds of choice.

» ¼-yard flower print fabric (backing)

» ⅛-yard red or gold fabric (insert border strips)

» ⅛-yard striped fabric (binding and hanging tab)

Cutting Plan

From the flower print, cut:
- one 8½" square for the backing

From the red or gold fabric, cut:
- one 1" x 42" insert border strip

From the striped fabric, cut:
- one 2¼" x 42" strip for the binding and hanging tab

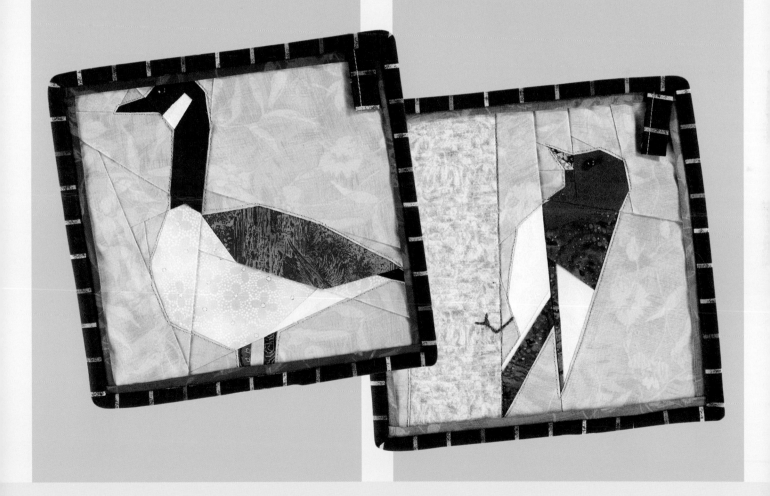

»»Decorate your kitchen with a flock of backyard bird potholders

requiring just one block each and some binding.««

Instructions

Note: All seam allowances are ¼" unless otherwise instructed.

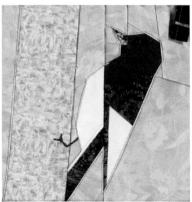

Step 1: As with the other projects in the book, you can vary the bird blocks in your potholder set as shown here, or make each potholder in the set exactly the same.

Assemble the Potholder Top

1. Paper-piece the bird block, following the instructions on pages 9 through 13, 134 or 143.

2. Press the 1"-wide red or gold insert border strip in half lengthwise (Figure 3-26). With raw edges even, baste the strip to one side edge of the bird block.

3. Trim the insert strip even with the top and bottom edges of the block (Figure 3-27).

4. Repeat steps 2 and 3 for the three remaining edges of the block.

5. Remove the paper from the bird block.

6. Hand stitch buttons or beads in place for the bird eyes and embroider the legs, if desired.

Finish the Potholder

1. Layer the potholder, following the instructions on page 16.

2. Quilt the block, outlining the bird.

3. Make binding for the block, following the instructions on pages 17 and 18.

Make the Hanging Tab

1. Topstitch the long open edges of a 3" piece of the binding together.

2. Fold the piece in half and baste to top of the potholder. Place the hanging tab at either a top corner or in the center.

3. Finish the binding, following the instructions on pages 17 and 18.

Figure 3-26

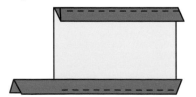

Figure 3-27

Family Room

Bring the outdoors in with these chirpily-cheery bird projects. The lap quilt will be welcomed during cold evenings, and the seasonal pillows can be switched out or celebrated all year long.

Lap Quilt

Finished size: 53" x 69"
Made by: Jodie Davis

Materials

See the large simple cardinal bird block on page 151 for fabric requirements, or select a different bird of choice.

» 4½ yards blue fabric (background)

» ⅛-yard gray fabric (birdhouse poles)

» 1 red fat quarter* (birdhouse)

» 2 beige fat quarters* (birdhouse)

» 9" x 4" scraps green, brown and dark gray fabrics (house trim and birds)

» ¼-yard dark blue fabric (inner border strips and binding)

» ½-yard green fabric (middle border and four corners)

» 6 yards striped fabric (outer border and backing)

» ⅜-yard each of two green fabrics (leaves)

» 60" x 75" piece batting

» 4 coverable 1½" to 1⅞" buttons (birdhouse holes)

» 4 black 1¾" x 2" scraps fabric (birdhouse holes)

» 1¼ yards braided trim or ribbon (sunflower stems)

» 13 assorted 6" squares brown fabrics (sunflower centers)

» 13 assorted 8½" x 22" pieces (approximately) yellow fabrics (sunflower petals)

» 3 black ¼" buttons or beads (bird eyes)

» Coordinating thread

» Glue stick

» Freezer paper

» Birdhouse, sunflower and simple cardinal piecing patterns (pages 71 through 77)

*Note: A fat quarter measures 18" x 21".

Cutting Plan

From the blue background fabric, cut:
- two 1¼" x 7¾" pieces for Birdhouse 1
- two 1¼" x 1½" top section pieces for Birdhouse 2
- two 1¼" x 4" top section pieces for Birdhouse 2
- two 1¼" x 7¼" bottom section pieces for Birdhouse 2
- two 1¾" x 9¼" pieces for Birdhouse 3
- 13 2½" x 14" strips and then cut each strip into four 2½" x 3½" pieces for each sunflower
- 2" x 6" "A" piece
- 3½" x 10" "B" piece
- 4½" x 24" "C" piece
- 1¾" x 7½" "D" piece
- 3" x 8¾" "E" piece
- 5½" x 8¾" "F" piece
- 4¾" x 15" "H" piece
- 5" x 18" "I" piece
- 1½" x 7½" "J" piece
- 8½" x 14" "K" piece
- 4" x 21" "M" piece
- 1½" x 6" "N" piece
- 3½" x 9½" "O" piece
- 4½" x 5" "P" piece
- 4½" x 5" "R" piece
- 2½" x 7½" "S" piece
- 4½" x 4½" "T" piece
- 4½" x 4½" "V" piece

From the gray fabric for the birdhouse poles, cut:
- 1½" x 15" "G" piece
- 1½" x 21" "L" piece
- 1½" x 5" "Q" piece
- 1½" x 4½" "U" piece

From the red fabric, cut:
- one 7½" x 9¼" body piece for Birdhouse 3
- one 7½" x 5" roof piece for Birdhouse 3

From the beige fabric, cut:
- one 8½" x 7¾" piece for Birdhouse 1
- one 4" x 5" top section piece for Birdhouse 2
- one 7" x 7¼" bottom section piece for Birdhouse 2

From the dark gray fabric, cut:
- one 1¼" x 6½" top section roof piece for Birdhouse 2
- one 1¼" x 8½" bottom section roof piece for Birdhouse 2

From the dark blue fabric, cut:
- two 1½" x 52½" side inner border strips
- two 1½" x 37½" top and bottom inner border strips

From the green fabric, cut:
- two 2½" x 54½" side middle border strips
- two 2½" x 41½" top and bottom middle border strips
- four 6½" square cornerstones

From the striped fabric, cut:
- two 6½" x 58½" side outer border strips
- two 6½" x 40" top and bottom outer border strips

»»Summer is in full bloom in this quilt of nesting birds and sunflowers raising their faces to the sun. Just the right size to snuggle up under on cool evenings, this quilt features inserted three-dimensional leaves in the sunflowers for a super fun effect.««

Quilt Layout/Cutting Plan Key

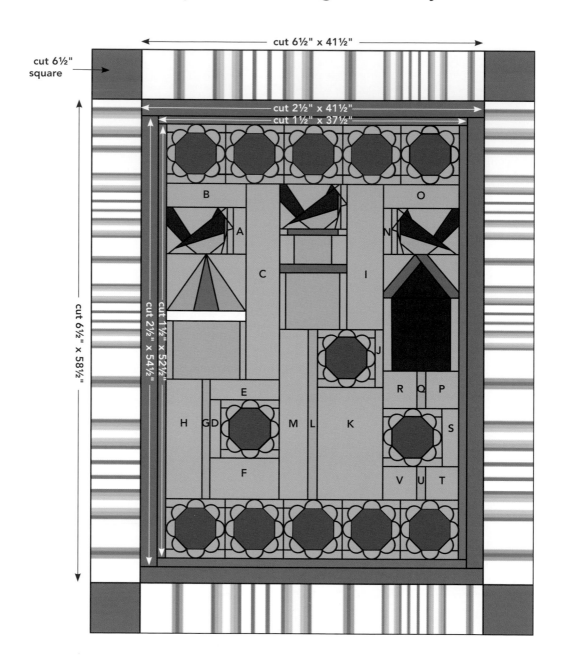

Tip

Place a small sticky note with the appropriate letter on each piece. It will make identifying them later much faster.

Quilt Layout/Cutting Plan Key

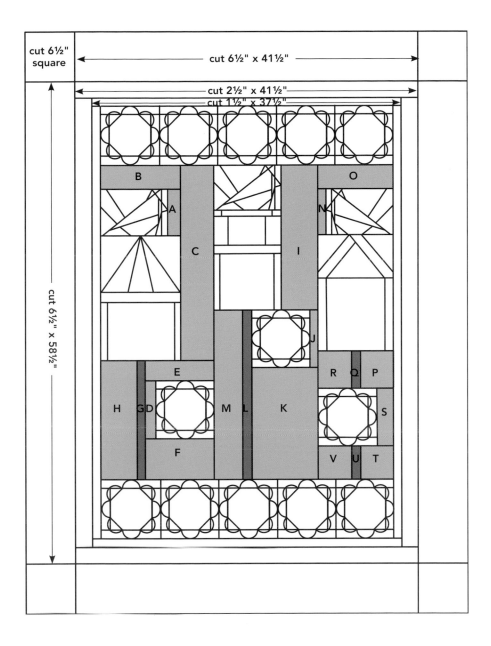

Step 1: Even though a simple cardinal pattern is used for each bird in this quilt, you can vary the colors used in the birds to get a different look, as shown here.

Instructions

Note: All seam allowances are ¼" unless otherwise instructed.

Assemble the Blocks

Refer to the layout diagram on the previous page, if necessary, while assembling the quilt top.

1. Make two right-facing bird blocks and one left-facing bird block, using the patterns on pages 73 and 74 and following the paper-piecing instructions on page 149.

BIRDHOUSE 1 (GREEN-PEAKED ROOF)

1. Make the roof section, following the paper-piecing pattern on page 71.

2. Stitch one blue 1¼" x 7¾" piece to each 7¾" side of the beige birdhouse piece. Press the seam allowances.

3. Stitch the birdhouse body to the paper-pieced birdhouse roof (Figures 4-1 and 4-2).

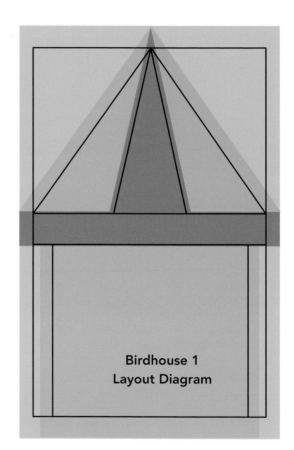

Birdhouse 1
Layout Diagram

Figure 4-1

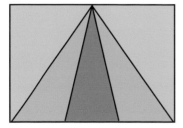

Figure 4-2

 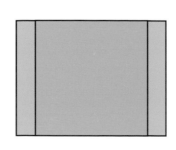

BIRDHOUSE 2 (DOUBLE-DECKER BIRDHOUSE)

1. For the top section, stitch the 1¼" edge of the two smaller blue top section pieces to each end of the gray roof piece (Figure 4-3).

2. Stitch the 4"-long edges of the two larger blue top section pieces to the matching edges of the beige top section piece (Figure 4-4).

3. Stitch the dark gray roof to the top edge of the beige top section piece (Figure 4-5). Set aside.

4. For the bottom section, stitch the two blue bottom section pieces to the longer edges of the beige bottom section piece (Figure 4-6).

5. Stitch the gray roof piece to the bottom section.

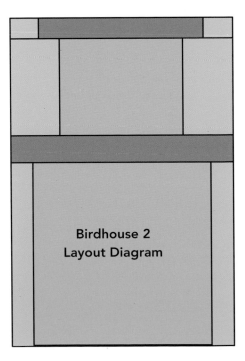

Figure 4-3

Figure 4-4

Figure 4-5

Figure 4-6

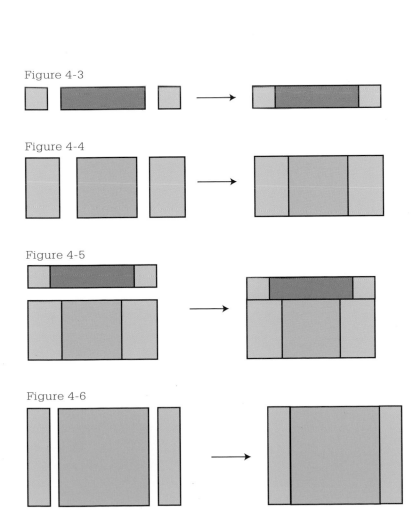

**Birdhouse 2
Layout Diagram**

BIRDHOUSE 3 (RED WITH GRAY ROOF)

1. Make the top section of the birdhouse, following the paper-piecing pattern on page 72.

2. Stitch the blue background pieces to the long edges of the red body piece (Figure 4-7). Press the seams open.

3. Stitch the birdhouse body to the paper-pieced birdhouse roof.

Figure 4-7

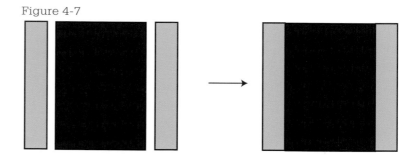

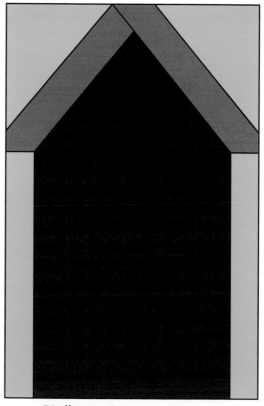

Birdhouse 3 Layout Diagram

SUNFLOWERS

1. Make 13 copies of the sunflower piecing pattern on page 75 and one copy of the sunflower center template on page 76.

2. Trace the sunflower petal patterns onto the non-smooth side of freezer paper, making a total of 13 sheets of petals.

3. For each of the 13 yellow fabrics, press the shiny side of the freezer paper to the wrong side of the fabric rectangle, positioning it to take up half of the rectangle. Fold fabric so you have two layers.

4. Stitch on the inner, solid curved lines (Figure 4-8).

5. Cut along the straight, bottom dashed lines of the petal patterns (Figure 4-9), cutting straight across the yardage.

6. Tear the paper from outside of the petal (Figure 4-10).

7. Trim the seam allowance at the top of the curve to about ⅛" (Figure 4-11).

Figure 4-8

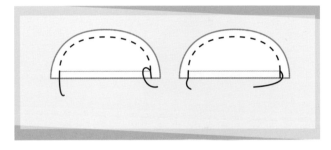

Figure 4-9

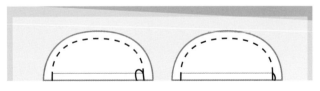

Figure 4-10

Figure 4-11

Tip

For step 2 » To print on freezer paper using an ink-jet printer, cut the freezer paper into 8½" x 11" pieces and press the shiny side onto regular paper. It feeds right through; just make sure you feed it through so the correct side will get printed. Remove the regular printer paper from the freezer paper.

Figure 4-12

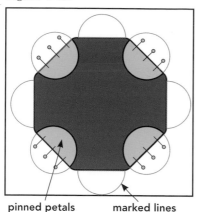

pinned petals   marked lines

Figure 4-13

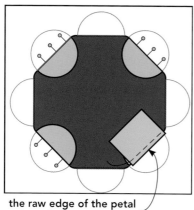

the raw edge of the petal
pieces butts on this line

8. Remove the paper from inside the petal and turn right-side out.

9. Machine baste the petals along their straight bottom edges just less than ¼" from the bottom raw edges.

10. Use the sunflower center cutting template on page 76 to cut out 13 brown sunflower centers.

11. Use a glue stick to lightly tack the sunflower centers to the unmarked side of the sunflower paper-piecing patterns, covering the area marked for Patch 1.

12. Place one printed pattern with a glued-on center on a clear table over the fluorescent light and pin the four corner petals in place (Figure 4-12), pulling up on the gather threads so the fabric half circle matches and completes the one on paper, with the raw edges of the petal matching those of the brown fabric.

13. Turn the pattern over to stitch along the lines and use the 2½" x 3½" blue pieces to paper-piece the corner background patches 2, 3,4. and5. (Figures 4-13 and 4-14). Be sure to remove each pin before you get to it. (Note: This is plain old paper-piecing; you just have the petal in-between!) Press the blue background in place.

14. As you did for the first four petals, pin the remaining four petals in place on the unmarked side of the paper.

15. Turn the paper over and paper-piece sections of the blue fabric strip, cut roughly 8" long for patches 6 and 7 (Figure 4-15). Press into place. Add patches 8 and 9 the same way. Press in place. Trim the block.

16. Trim the block (Figure 4-16).

Note: In Figures 4-12 through 4-16, the fabric is shown from the right side, not the side you sew from.

Figure 4-14

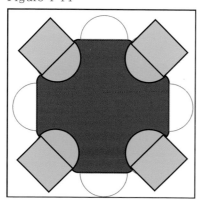

Figure 4-15

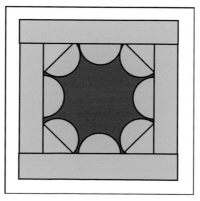

Figure 4-16

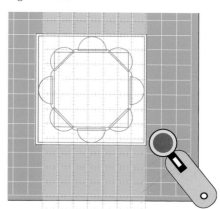

ASSEMBLE THE SECTIONS

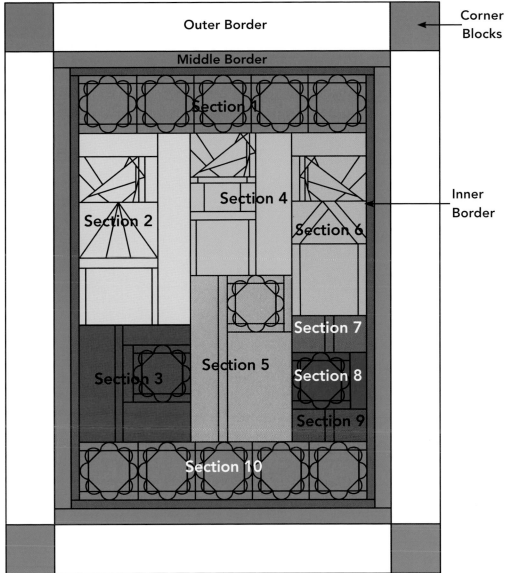

Section Assembly Guide

Corner Blocks

Outer Border

Middle Border

Section 1

Section 4

Inner Border

Section 2

Section 6

Section 7

Section 5

Section 3

Section 8

Section 9

Section 10

Complete the eight sections of the quilt as follows, pressing seams to one side or open as you go. Refer to the Section Assembly Guide as you assemble the sections, if necessary.

Sections 1 and 10 (Figure 4-17; one row equals one section)

1. Stitch two rows of five sunflower blocks each.

Figure 4-17

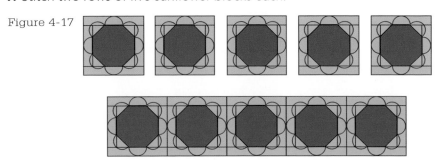

Section 2 (Figure 4-18)

1. Stitch A to the beak side of a right-facing cardinal block.

2. Stitch B to the top of the cardinal block. Press.

3. Stitch Birdhouse 1 to the bottom of the block.

4. Stitch C to the right side of the block.

Section 3 (Figure 4-19)

1. Stitch D to what will be the left side of a sunflower block.

2. Stitch E to the top of the block.

3. Stitch F to the bottom of the block.

4. Stitch G to the left side of the block.

5. Stitch H to the left side of the block.

Section 4 (Figure 4-20)

1. Stitch the second right-facing cardinal block to the top of Birdhouse 2.

2. Stitch I to the right side of the block.

Figure 4-18

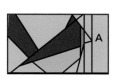
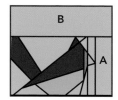
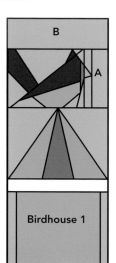
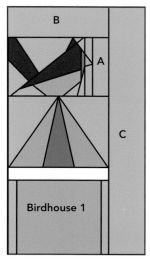

Figure 4-19

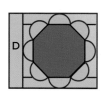
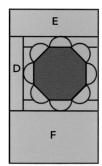
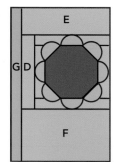
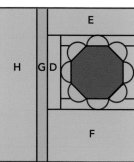

Figure 4-20

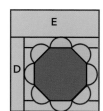

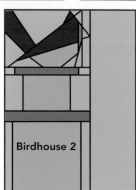

Section 5 (Figure 4-21)

1. Stitch J to the right side of a sunflower block.

2. Stitch K to the bottom of the block.

3. Stitch L to the left side of the block. Press.

4. Stitch M to the left side of the block.

Section 6 (Figure 4-22)

1. Stitch N to the left side of the left-facing cardinal block.

2. Stitch O to the top of the block.

3. Stitch Birdhouse 3. to the bottom of the block.

Section 7 (Figure 4-23)

1. Stitch P to Q, matching the 5"-long sides.

2. Stitch R to Q, matching the 5"-long sides.

Section 8 (Figure 4-24)

1. Stitch S to the right side of the remaining sunflower block.

Section 9 (Figure 4-25)

1. Stitch T to U, matching the 4½"-long sides.

2. Stitch V to U.

Figure 4-21

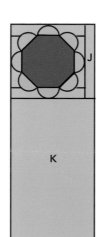
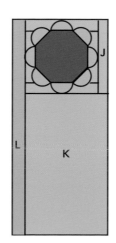
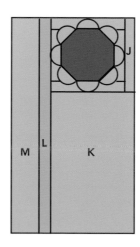

Figure 4-22

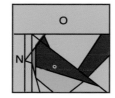

Figure 4-23

Figure 4-24

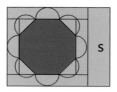

Figure 4-25

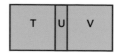

Assemble the Quilt Top

1. Stitch Section 2. to the top of Section 3. (Figure 4-26).

2. Stitch Section 4. to the top of Section 5. (Figure 4-27).

3. Stitch Section 7 to the bottom of Section 6 (Figure 4-28).

4. Stitch Section 8 to the bottom of Section 7 (Figure 4-29).

5. Stitch Section 9 to the bottom of Section 8 (Figure 4-30).

6. Stitch the three strips of sections together (Figure 4-31).

7. Stitch one row of sunflowers to the top of the quilt and stitch the other row of sunflowers to the bottom (Figure 4-32).

INNER BORDER

1. Stitch the dark blue side inner border strips to the sides of the quilt top (Figure 4-33). Press seam allowances toward the quilt top.

2. Stitch the dark blue top and bottom inner border strips to the top and bottom of the quilt top (Figure 4-34). Press the seam allowances toward the quilt top.

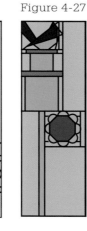

Figure 4-26 Figure 4-27

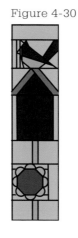

Figure 4-28 Figure 4-29 Figure 4-30

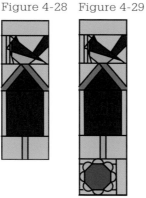

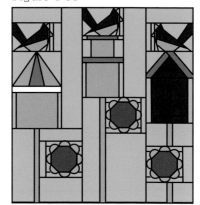

Figure 4-31

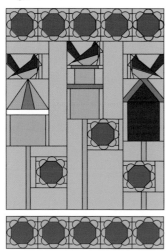

Figure 4-32

Figure 4-33

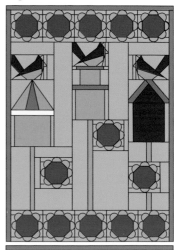

Figure 4-34

MIDDLE BORDER

1. Stitch green side middle border strips to the sides of the quilt top (Figure 4-35). Press the seam allowances toward the quilt top.

2. Stitch the green top and bottom middle border strips to the top and bottom of the quilt top (Figure 4-36). Press the seam allowances toward the quilt top.

Figure 4-35

Figure 4-36

OUTER BORDER

1. Stitch the striped side outer border strips to the sides of the quilt top (Figure 4-37). Press the seam allowances toward the quilt top.

2. Stitch the green corner squares to the ends of the remaining striped border strips. Press the seam allowances to one side.

3. Stitch the strips to the top and bottom of the quilt top (Figure 4-38). Press the seam allowances toward the quilt top.

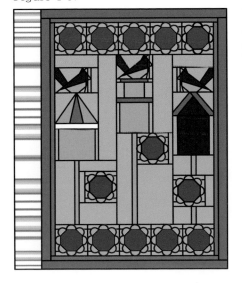

Figure 4-37

Figure 4-38

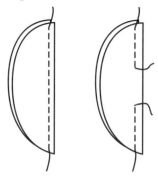

Figure 4-39

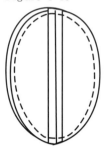

Figure 4-40

Embellish the Quilt Top

1. Pair up the green leaf pieces into 14 sets, using one of each of the greens in each set.

2. Match and stitch the straight edges with right sides together (Figure 4-39). For half of them, leave a 2"-long gap in the stitching, as shown, for turning. Press the seam allowances open.

3. Pair up the sets so the fabrics alternate and stitch, with right sides together, all the way around the outside of each leaf (Figure 4-40).

4. Turn the leaves right-side out.

5. Stitch them to the quilt top along their center seam lines with open seam toward the top.

Finish the Quilt

1. Remove the paper from the blocks.

2. Hand stitch the braided trim or ribbon to the quilt top for the sunflower stems.

3. Remove the selvedges from the backing and cut the backing into two 2¼-yard lengths.

4. Seam them together along one long edge.

5. Layer, quilt and bind the quilt, following the instructions on pages 16 through 18. Note the quilting in the photos here and use the design as a guide, if you wish.

6. Cover the buttons with dark brown fabric scraps.

7. Sew the buttons to the birdhouses for the openings.

8. Hand stitch buttons or beads in place for the bird eyes.

9. Press the sunflower petals open.

make 1

Birdhouse 1
Roof Piecing Pattern

Note: Add a ¼" seam allowance all the way around this pattern.

Birdhouse 3 Roof Piecing Pattern

make 1

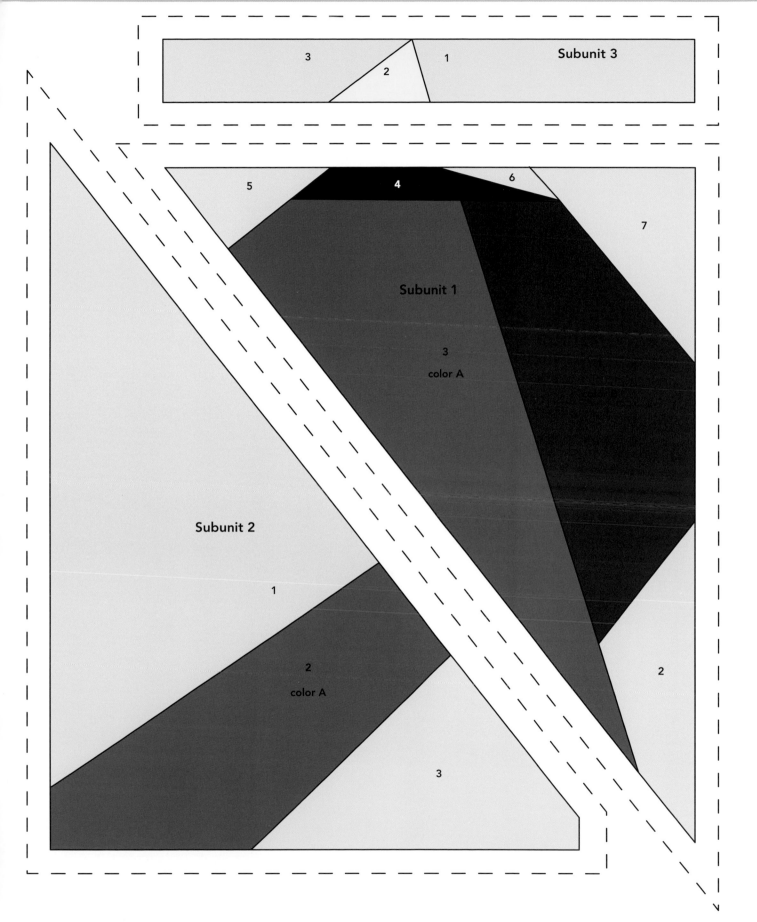

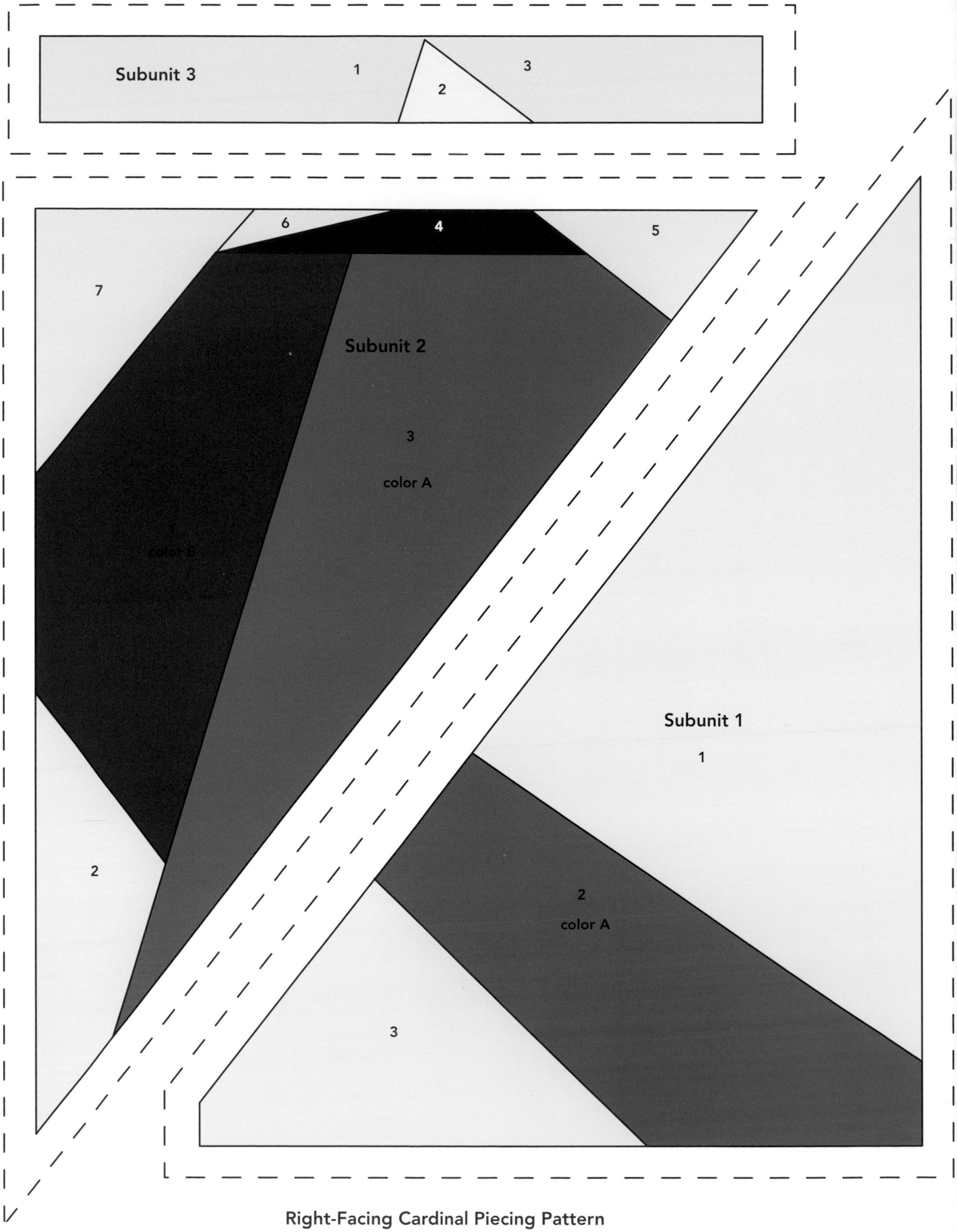

Subunit 3

1

2

3

6

4

5

7

Subunit 2

3

color A

1

color B

Subunit 1

1

2

2

color A

3

Right-Facing Cardinal Piecing Pattern

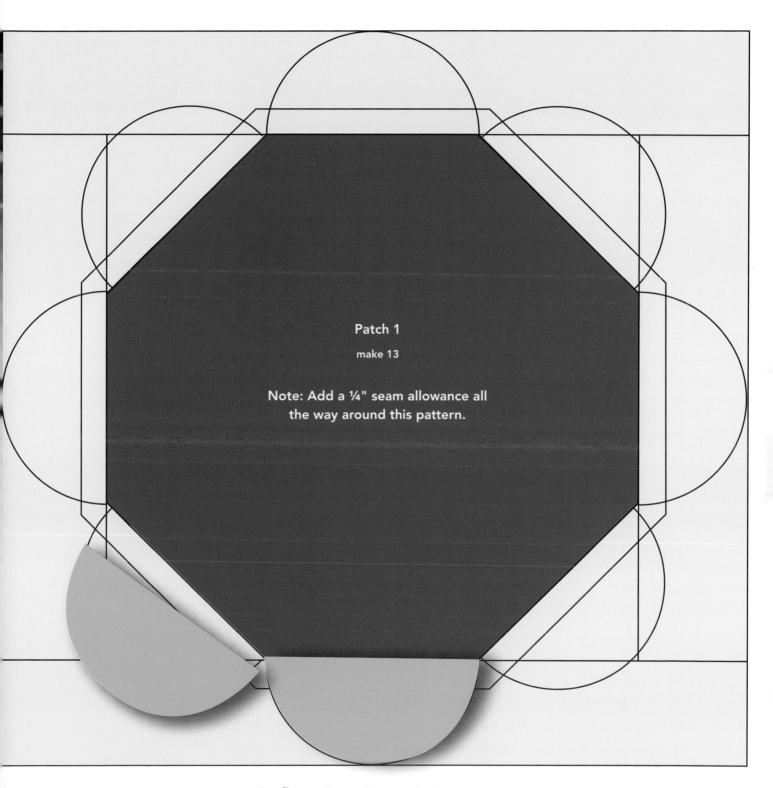

Patch 1

make 13

Note: Add a ¼" seam allowance all the way around this pattern.

Sunflower Paper-Piecing Pattern

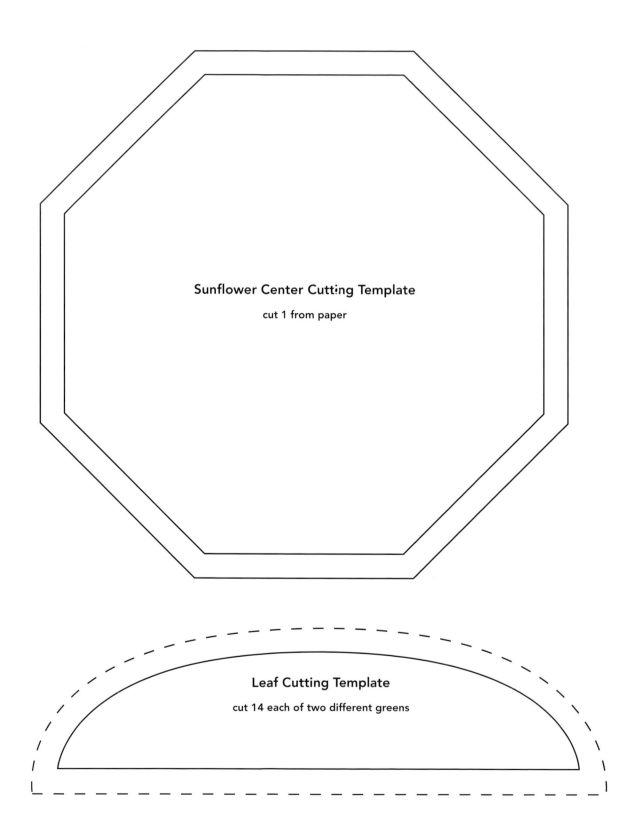

Sunflower Center Cutting Template

cut 1 from paper

Leaf Cutting Template

cut 14 each of two different greens

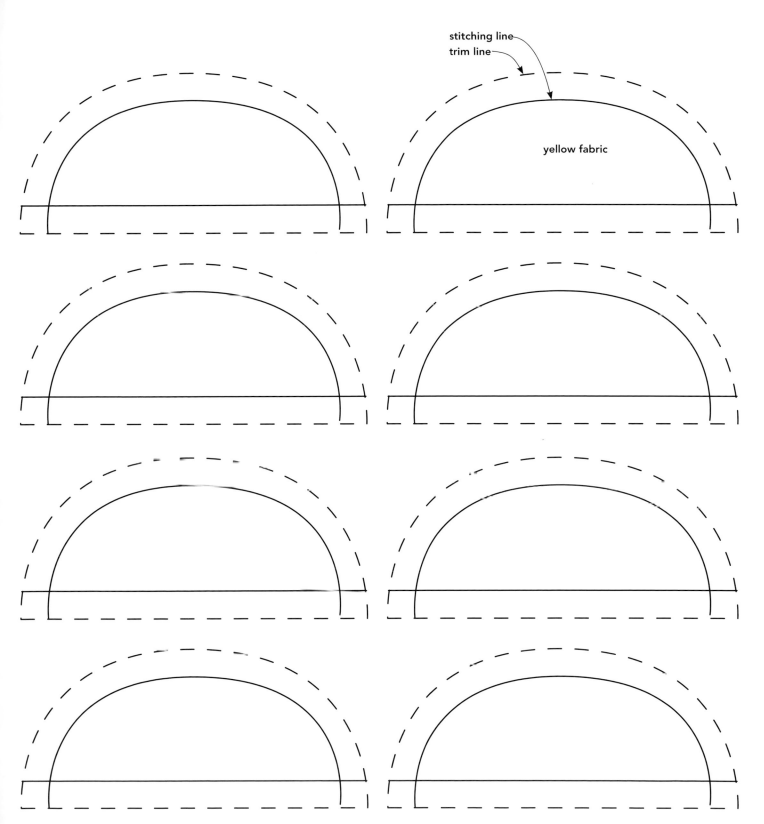

stitching line
trim line
yellow fabric

Sunflower Petals Cutting Template

make 1 sheet per sunflower (13 sheets total)

Spring Pillow

Finished size: 18" square plus pompom fringe
Made by: Jodie Davis

Materials

See the wren bird block on page 121 for fabric requirements, or select a different bird of choice.

» ⅝-yard striped fabric
(inner borders and backing)

» ½-yard green fabric
(insert border strips and outer borders)

» 2 4½ squares blue scrap fabric (flower appliqué)

» 4 4½ squares white scrap fabric (flower appliqué)

» 2 4½ squares green scrap fabric (leaf appliqué)

» 1½ yards white pompom fringe

» 6 white 4mm beads

» 18" pillow form

» Coordinating thread

» Spring Pillow Flower pattern
(page 81)

» Spring Pillow Leaf pattern
(page 81)

Cutting Plan

From the striped fabric, cut:
- four 5"-wide inner border strips
- two 12½" x 18½" pillow backing pieces

From the green fabric, cut:
- one 1" x 42" insert border strip
- two 1½" x 17½" side outer border strips
- two 1½" x 18½" top and bottom outer border strips

»»The pretty three-dimensional flowers and perky white pompom fringe make this pillow as cheerful as a spring day. To take advantage of the stripe in the border fabric I chose, I sewed the border on with mitered corners.««

Step 1

Figure 4-42

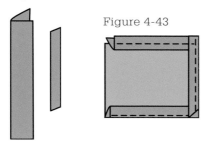

Figure 4-43

Figure 4-44

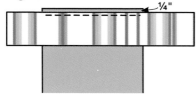

Figure 4-45

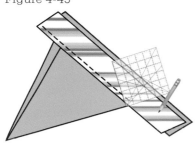

Figure 4-46

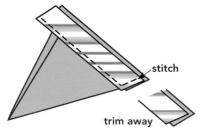

stitch

trim away

Instructions

Note: All seam allowances are ¼" unless otherwise instructed.

Assemble the Pillow Top

Refer to the layout diagram on the next page, if necessary, while assembling the pillow top.

1. Paper-piece the bird block, following the instructions on page 118.

2. Press the 1"-wide green insert border strip in half lengthwise (Figure 4-42).

3. Baste the green insert strip to one side edge of the bird block, with raw edges even and trim the insert strip even with the top and bottom edges of the block. Repeat for the three remaining edges of the block (Figure 4-43).

4. Center a striped inner border strip on one raw edge of the bird block and stitch in place (Figure 4-44), stopping and starting ¼" from the edge. **Note:** The line on the paper makes an excellent guide. Repeat for all three edges and border strips. Press the seam allowances toward the border.

5. Fold the pillow top in half diagonally so the edges of the bird block match and form a triangle and pin the raw edges of the border strips together.

6. Use a 45-degree ruler to mark a sewing line (Figure 4-45) and stitch along that line (Figure 4-46).

7. Trim the seam allowance and press open.

8. Repeat steps 6 and 7 for the remaining three corners.

9. Stitch a green side outer border strip to each side of the pillow top (Figure 4-47). Press the seam allowances toward the border.

10. Stitch a green top and bottom outer border strip to the top and bottom of the pillow (Figure 4-48).

11. Baste the pompom fringe to the wrong side of the pillow top, all around the four sides.

12. On one long edge of each pillow backing, press under ¼" and then press under another 1".

13. Topstitch the hem in place.

Figure 4-47

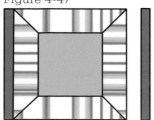

Figure 4-48

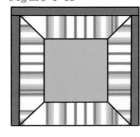

Finish the Pillow

Note: You may find it easier to add your appliqué embellishment before you finish the pillow by stitching the pillow top and back pieces together. If you do embellish first, be sure to place the appliqué flower and leaves far enough from the corner, so they do not extend into the outer seam allowance.

1. Remove the paper from the bird block.

2. Lay the pillow top and backing with right sides together on a flat surface, pin carefully, making sure the pompoms stay in place, and stitch all the way around (Figure 4-49).

3. Turn the pillow right-side out and insert the pillow form.

Embellish the Pillow

1. Cut two pieces of fabric for each appliqué at least ½" larger than you need all around.

2. Trace the pattern onto the wrong side of one piece of fabric.

3. Lay the piece with the pattern right-side down on top the other piece and stitch along the traced lines (Figure 4-50).

4. Trim the seam allowance to about ⅛" (Figure 4-51).

5. Make a slit in one layer of fabric and turn the appliqué right-side out.

6. Repeat steps 1 through 5 for the remaining flower and leaf appliqué pieces.

7. Stitch the appliqués to the pillow top, starting first with the leaves and then adding the flower petals, scrunching up the blue flower a bit when you sew it down, as shown (Figure 4-52).

8. Hand stitch the beads to the center of the flower for the finished look shown at right.

Figure 4-49

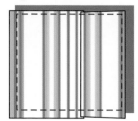

Figure 4-50

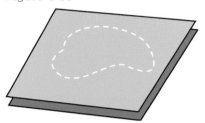

Figure 4-51

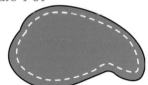

Figure 4-52

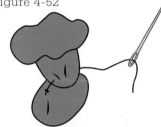

Step 8

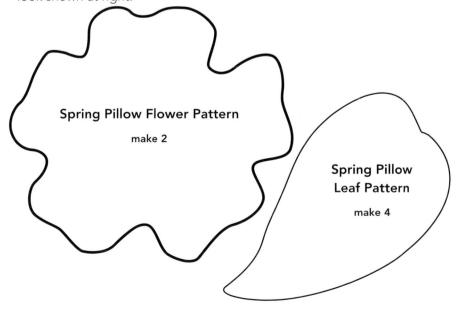

Spring Pillow Flower Pattern

make 2

Spring Pillow Leaf Pattern

make 4

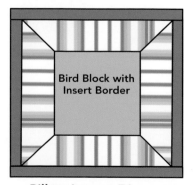

Bird Block with Insert Border

Pillow Layout Diagram

Summer Pillow

Finished size: 18" square plus fringe
Made by: Jodie Davis

Materials

See the hummingbird block on page 125 for fabric requirements, or select a different bird of choice.

» ⅝-yard blue print fabric (borders and backing)

» 1½ yards each of two fuzzy fringe trims

» 18" pillow form*

» Coordinating thread

*Used in this project: Mountain Mist's A Touch of Silk

Cutting Plan

From the blue fabric, cut:
- two 5½" x 8½" side border pieces
- two 5½" x 18½" top and bottom border pieces
- two 12½" x 18½" pillow backing pieces

»»Purchased fuzzy trim frames this pillow and reflects the texture of the bird feathers. Indulge yourself with a luxury pillow form to complement this luxurious pillow cover.««

Instructions

Note: All seam allowances are ¼" unless otherwise instructed.

Step 1

Assemble the Pillow Top

Refer to the layout diagram below, if necessary, while assembling the pillow top.

1. Paper-piece the bird block, following the instructions on pages 9 through 13 and 125.

2. Stitch a side border piece to each side of the bird block (Figure 4-53). Press the seam allowances toward the border.

3. Stitch the top and bottom border pieces to the top and bottom of the block (Figure 4-54). Press the seam allowances toward the border.

4. Baste the two layers of fringe to the right side of the pillow top, all the way around (Figure 4-55). Trim.

5. On one long edge of each pillow backing, press under ¼" and then press under another 1".

6. Topstitch the hem in place.

Finish the Pillow

1. Remove the paper from the bird block.

2. Place the pillow top and pillow back with right sides together on a flat surface, pin carefully with the fringe inside the pillow layers and stitch all the way around.

3. Turn the pillow right-side out and insert the pillow form.

Figure 4-53

Figure 4-54

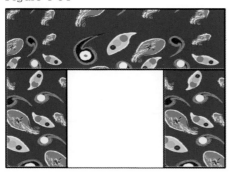

Figure 4-55

Bird Block with
Insert Border

Fall Pillow

Finished size: 18" square
Made by: Jodie Davis

Materials

See the towhee bird block on page 118 for fabric requirements, or select a different bird of choice.

» ¼-yard leafy brown fabric (inner borders)

» ½-yard brown print fabric (insert border strips, outer borders and backing)

» 4 4½ squares brown scrap fabric

» 4 4½ squares alternate brown/beige scrap fabric

» 18" pillow form

» Coordinating thread

» Fall Leaf A pattern (page 88)

» Fall Leaf B pattern (page 88)

Cutting Plan

From the leafy brown fabric, cut
- two 4½" x 8½" side inner border pieces
- two 4½" x 16½" top and bottom inner border pieces

From the brown print fabric, cut:
- two 1½" x 17½" side outer border strips
- two 1½" x 18½" top and bottom outer border strips
- one 1" x 42" insert border strip
- two 12½" x 18½" pillow backing pieces »«

»»You will smell the crisp autumn air when you bring out this leafy pillow. To spice up the appliqués, add beads or use metallic thread to stitch them down.««

Instructions

Note: All seam allowances are ¼" unless otherwise instructed.

Assemble the Pillow Top

Refer to the layout diagram on page 88, if necessary, while assembling the pillow top.

1. Paper-piece the bird block, following the instructions on pages 9 through 13 and 118.

2. Press the 1"-wide brown print insert border strip in half lengthwise (Figure 4-56).

3. With raw edges even, baste the strip to one side edge of the bird block and trim the insert strip even with the top and bottom edges of the block. Repeat for the three remaining edges of the block.

4. Stitch the side inner border pieces to the sides of the bird block (Figure 4-57). Press the seam allowances toward the border.

5. Stitch the top and bottom inner border pieces to the top and bottom of the block (Figure 4-58). Press the seam allowances toward the border.

6. Stitch the side outer border piece to each side of the bird block (Figure 4-59). Press the seam allowances toward the border.

7. Stitch the top and bottom outer border pieces to the top and bottom of the block (Figure 4-60). Press the seam allowances toward the border.

8. On one long edge of each pillow backing, press under ¼" and then press under another 1". Topstitch the hem in place.

Step 1

Figure 4-56

Figure 4-57

Figure 4-58

Figure 4-59

Figure 4-60

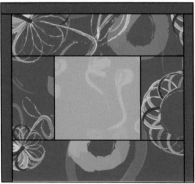

Step 7

Pillow Layout Diagram

Finish the Pillow

Note: You may find it easier to add your appliqué embellishment before you finish the pillow by stitching the pillow top and back pieces together. If you do embellish first, be sure to place the appliqué leaves far enough from the corner, so they do not extend into the outer seam allowance.

1. Remove the paper from the bird block.

2. Lay the pillow top and pillow back right sides together on a flat surface and stitch all the way around.

3. Turn the pillow right-side out and insert the pillow form.

Embellish the Pillow

1. Cut two pieces of fabric for each appliqué at least ½" larger than the pattern all around.

2. Trace the pattern onto the wrong side of one piece of fabric.

3. Lay the piece with the pattern right-side down on top of the other piece and stitch along the traced lines. (For illustrated assistance with this step, see Figure 4-50 in the Spring Pillow project, page 81.)

4. Trim the seam allowance to about ⅛". (For illustrated assistance with this step, see Figure 4-51 in the Spring Pillow project, page 81.)

5. Make a slit in one layer of fabric and turn the appliqué right-side out.

6. Repeat steps 1 through 5 for the three remaining leaf appliqués.

7. Stitch the appliqués to the pillow top, along the centers of the leaves to simulate veins for the finished look, as shown above left.

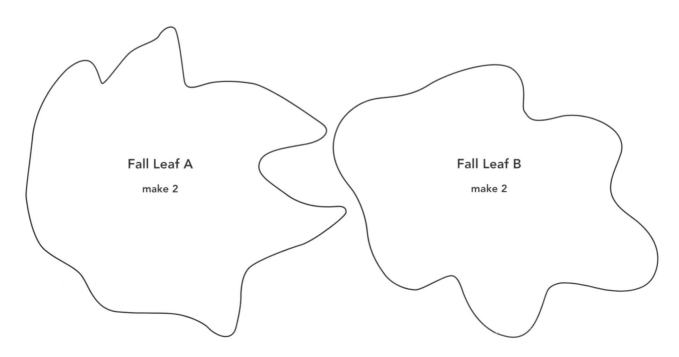

Fall Leaf A

make 2

Fall Leaf B

make 2

Winter Pillow

Finished size: 18" square
Made by: Jodie Davis

Materials

See the cardinal bird block on page 115 for fabric requirements, or select a different bird of choice.

» ¼-yard blue batik fabric (inner borders)

» ¼-yard blue print fabric (middle borders)

» ⅝-yard blue striped fabric (outer borders and backing)

» ⅛-yard blue-and-red fabric (insert border strips)

» 1 package size 7mm white pompoms

» 18" pillow form

» Coordinating thread

» 1 small bead or button (bird eye)

Cutting Plan

From the blue batik fabric, cut:
- two 2½" x 8½" side inner border pieces
- two 2½" x 12½" top and bottom inner border pieces

From the blue print fabric, cut:
- two 2½" x 12½" side middle border strips
- two 2½" x 16½" top and bottom middle border strips

From the blue striped fabric, cut:
- two 1½" x 16½" side outer border strips
- two 1½" x 18½" top and bottom outer border strips
- two 12½" x 18½" pillow backing pieces

From the blue-and-red fabric, cut:
- one 1" x 42" insert border strip

»»A familiar sight in winter, cardinals perch in a light snow, but this pillow's snow is a warm and fuzzy flurry of tiny pompoms!««

Instructions

Note: All seam allowances are ¼" unless otherwise instructed.

Assemble the Pillow Top

Refer to the layout diagram on page 92, if necessary, while assembling the pillow top.

1. Paper-piece the bird block, following the instructions on pages 9 through 13 and 115.

Figure 4-62

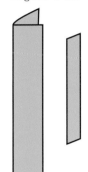

2. Press the blue batik insert border strip in half lengthwise (Figure 4-61).

3. With raw edges even, baste the strip to one side edge of the bird block and trim the insert strip even with the top and bottom edges of the block. Repeat for the three remaining edges of the block.

4. Stitch the side inner border pieces to the sides of the bird block (Figure 4-62). Press the seam allowances toward the border.

5. Stitch the top and bottom inner border pieces to the top and bottom of the block (Figure 4-63). Press the seam allowances toward the border.

6. Stitch the side middle border strips to the sides of the bird block (Figure 4-64). Press the seam allowances toward the border.

7. Stitch the top and bottom middle border strips to the top and bottom of the block (Figure 4-65). Press the seam allowances toward the border.

8. Stitch the side outer border strips to the sides of the bird block (Figure 4-66). Press the seam allowances toward the border.

9. Stitch the top and bottom outer border strips to the top and bottom of the block (Figure 4-67). Press the seam allowances toward the border.

Step 1

Figure 4-62

Figure 4-63

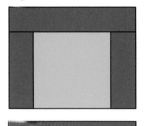

Figure 4-64

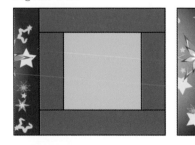

Figure 4-67

Figure 4-65

Figure 4-66

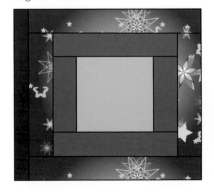

Embellish Step 2

Embellish the Pillow

1. Remove the paper from the bird block.

2. Hand stitch pompoms to the pillow top to simulate snow, as shown at left.

3. Add beads or buttons for the bird's eyes.

Finish the Pillow

1. Press under ¼" on one long edge of each pillow backing piece and then press under another 1". Topstitch the hem in place.

2. Lay the pillow top and pillow back right sides together on a flat surface and stitch all the way around.

3. Turn the pillow right-side out and insert the pillow form.

Bird Block with Insert Border

Pillow Layout Diagram

Bedroom Projects

Batiks are so easy to work with. They are delicacies for the eyes, always seem
to match and lend themselves well to birds. So, I chose to use them for a room
full of birds. Watercolor batiks, and those that are patterned and mottled, offer
plenty of material suitable for birds. A note to help you with the stripped blocks:
A square rotary cutting ruler will cut the stripped square blocks quickly.

Bed Quilt

Finished size: 88" x 104"
Made by: Joyce Woodall (bird block sewing) and
Mavis Rosbach (construction and quilting)

Materials

See each of the 12 main bird blocks on pages 112 through 146 for fabric requirements, or select a different bird of choice.

» 6 yards total of assorted green batik fabrics* (stripped blocks and binding)

» 1⅞ yards blue batik fabric* (inner borders and outer borders)

» 6½ yards green print fabric (backing)

» 88" x 104" batting (king-size)

*Used in this project: Hoffman Fabrics

Cutting Plan

From the blue batik fabric, cut:
- two 4½" x 72½" inner side border strips
- two 4½" x 64½" inner top and bottom border strips
- two 4½" x 96½" outer side border strips
- two 4½" x 88½" outer top and bottom outer strips

»»Sleep under a dreamy batik forest full of your favorite birds in this bed quilt made of batik fabrics. If you don't want beads on your quilt, embroider the bird eyes with French knots.««

Instructions

Note: All seam allowances are ¼" unless otherwise instructed.

Assemble the Blocks

Paper-piece the 12 main bird blocks, following the instructions on pages 9 through 13 and 112 through 146.

The 12 bird blocks coordinate well when the backgrounds, in this case blue, match not only each other, but also the blue batik used for the borders in the quilt top.

Stripped Blocks

1. Rotary cut each of the green folded fabrics from selvedges to fold into strips of random widths, forming wedge-shaped pieces varying between 1¼" to 5" wide at either end (Figure 5-1).

2. Cut the folded edges of each of the green batik wedge-shaped strips (Figure 5-2).

3. Stitch the strips together randomly. Press the seam allowances in one direction.

4. Use a square rotary ruler to cut the pieced strips into 8½" squares (Figure 5-3) for a yield of 91 squares.

Figure 5-1

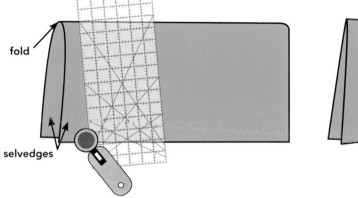
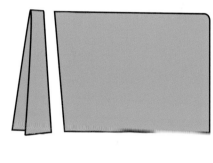

fold

selvedges

Figure 5-2

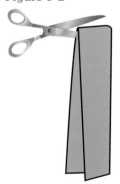

Figure 5-3

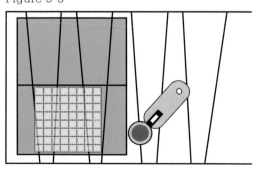

cut 8" squares

Assemble the Quilt Top

Refer to the layout diagram on the next page, if necessary, while assembling the quilt top.

1. Arrange the bird blocks and 51 of the stripped blocks as they will appear in the center of the finished quilt, following the bed quilt photo on page 95.

2. Start at the top left and stitch the blocks into rows. Press the seam allowances in one direction.

3. Start at the top and stitch the rows together (Figure 5-4). Press the seam allowances in one direction.

4. Stitch the inner side border strips to the sides of the quilt top (Figure 5-5).

5. Stitch the inner top and bottom border strips to the top and bottom edges of the quilt top (Figure 5-6).

6. Stitch the remaining 40 stripped blocks into four sets of 10 each to make the middle border.

7. Stitch a set of blocks to each long side edge of the quilt (Figure 5-7).

Figure 5-4

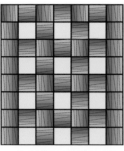

Figure 5-5

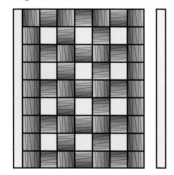

Figure 5-6

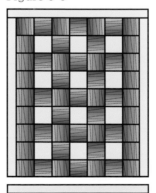

Figure 5-7

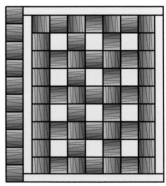

Figure 5-8

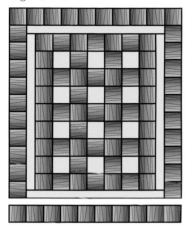

8. Stitch the remaining two sets to the top and bottom of the quilt (Figure 5-8).

9. Stitch the outer side border strips to the sides of the quilt top (Figure 5-9).

10. Stitch the outer top and bottom border strips to the top and bottom edges of the quilt top (Figure 5-10).

Finish the Quilt

1. Remove the paper from the bird blocks.

2. Layer, quilt and bind the quilt, following the instructions on pages 16 through 18.

Note: Mavis echo-quilted the birds, stitched along the striped block lines, and quilted a crosshatch in the blue batik borders.

Figure 5-9

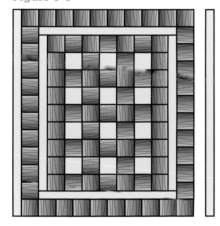

Figure 5-10

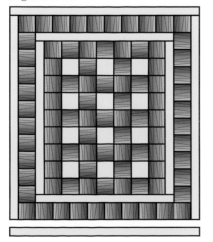

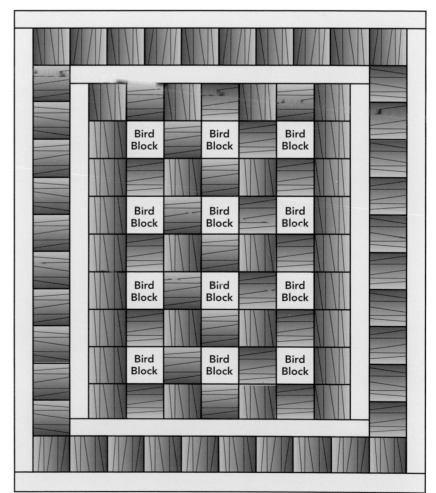

Bed Quilt Layout Diagram

Pillow Shams

Finished size: 24" x 34"
Made by: Mavis Rosbach

Materials
(for one sham)

» ½-yard green print fabric (pillow sham)

» ¼-yard each of eight green fabrics (tree blocks)

» 1¼ yards total assorted blue fabrics (tree blocks and tree border strips)

» 1½ yards lining fabric

» King-size bed pillow*

» Tree Piecing Pattern (page 103)

*Used in this project: Down Factory pillow

Cutting Plan
(for each placemat)

From the green print fabric, cut:
- one 23" x 48½" main sham piece

From the blue fabric, cut:
- one 8½" x 26½" tree border strip
- one 2½" x 8½" tree border strip

From the lining fabric, cut:
- one 39½" x 48½" lining panel

»»Complement your bird quilt with matching pillow shams.

Indulge yourself in the pleasure of real feather pillows.««

Instructions

Note: All seam allowances are ¼" unless otherwise instructed.

Assemble Step 1

Assemble the Pillow Sham Top

Refer to the layout diagram below, if necessary, while assembling the pillow sham top.

1. Paper-piece five tree blocks, following the instructions on the next page and pages 9 through 13.

2. Stitch the tree blocks into a row, side-by-side.

3. Stitch the 2½" x 8½" tree border strip to the left side of the strip of blocks.

4. Stitch the 8½" x 26½" tree border strip to the right side of the blocks (Figure 5-11).

5. Stitch the tree border strip to one long edge of the large green piece (Figure 5-12).

6. Stitch the long edge of the lining piece to the bottom of the tree border strip (Figure 5-13).

Finish the Pillow Sham

1. Remove the paper from the tree blocks.

2. Quilt straight horizontal lines on the large green section and then quilt the green portions of the tree blocks, as shown in Step 1 photo, above left.

3. Fold the sham in half lengthwise, right sides together, and sew the long edges together.

4. Fold the lining back over the sham. The right side of the lining is now facing out and quilted sham is inside. The lining fabric is larger than the sham top by 8", creating the 4" hem of the sham.

5. Make sure the quilted sham edges and lining are straight, pin and sew through all four layers on remaining raw edge.

6. Turn the sham right-side out.

7. To make an enclosed seam, stitch another ¼" seam. Turn wrong-side out and stitch another seam. Turn right-side out.

Figure 5-11

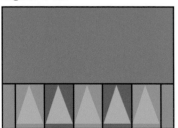

Figure 5-12

Figure 5-13

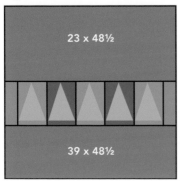

23 x 48½

39 x 48½

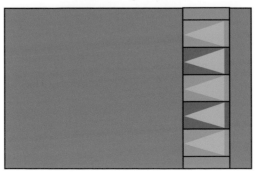

Pillow Sham Layout Diagram

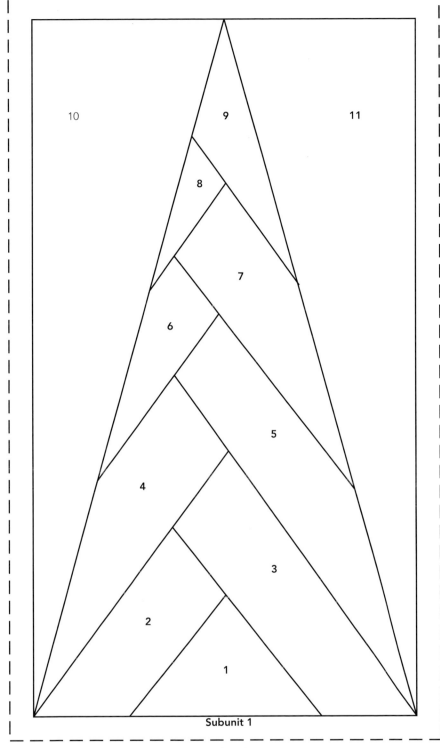

Tree Piecing Pattern

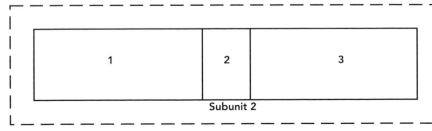

Tree Block Piecing Pattern

Fabric Requirements*

- Scraps of green fabrics to total approximately 8" square (tree body)

- 4" x 10" piece blue fabric (background)

- 1½" square brown fabric (tree trunk)

*Fabric requirements are estimates. Due to the paper-piecing method, you may use more or less.

Piecing Instructions

Subunit piecing order; sew as follows:

Subunit 1 to 2.

Quilted Headboard

Finished size: 24" x 56"
Made by: Mavis Rosbach

Materials

» 1¾ yards assorted green fabrics (binding and stripped blocks; ¼-yard cuts of eight fabrics works well)

» 1¼ yards assorted green fabrics (tree blocks)

» 1 yard blue batik fabric (tree blocks)

» 13 brown 2" scraps fabrics (tree blocks)

» 1¾ yard backing fabric

» Batting

» Tree Piecing Pattern (page 103)

Cutting Plan

From any of assorted green fabrics, cut:
• two 2½" x 8½" binding strips
• one 8" x 54" strip (hanging sleeve)

»»This headboard is a perfect backdrop

for your bird quilt and pillow shams.««

Instructions

Note: All seam allowances are ¼" unless otherwise instructed.

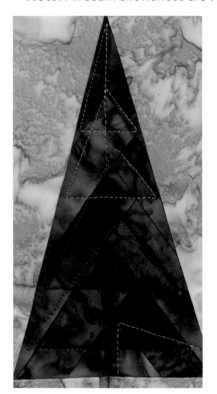

Assemble the Tree Blocks

Paper-piece 13 tree blocks as shown in the photo at left, following the instructions on pages 9 through 13 and 103.

Assemble the Stripped Blocks

1. Rotary cut each of the green folded fabrics from selvedges to fold into strips or random widths, forming wedge-shaped pieces varying between 1¼" to 5" wide at either end (Figure 5-14).

2. Cut the folded edges of each of the green wedge-shaped strips (Figure 5-15).

3. Stitch the strips together randomly. Press the seam allowances in one direction.

4. Use a square rotary ruler to cut the strips into 8½" squares (Figure 5-16) for a yield of 14 squares.

Figure 5-14

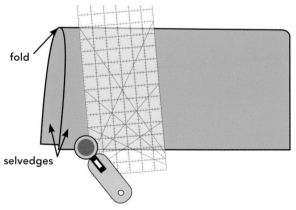

fold

selvedges

Figure 5-15

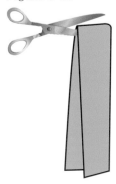

Figure 5-16

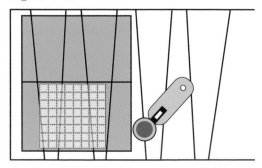

Assemble the Headboard Top

Refer to the layout diagram below, if necessary, while assembling the headboard top.

1. Arrange the tree blocks and stripped blocks as they will appear in the finished quilt, referring to the Headboard Layout Diagram below. The green strips go at the ends of the middle row.

2. Start at the top left and stitch the blocks into rows first (top, middle and bottom rows). Press the seam allowances in one direction.

3. Stitch the rows to each other; first top row to middle row and then the top-middle unit to bottom row. Press the seam allowances in one direction.

Finish the Headboard

1. Remove the paper from the blocks.

2. Layer, quilt and bind, following the instructions on pages 16 through 18.

3. Make a hanging sleeve, following the instructions on page 16.

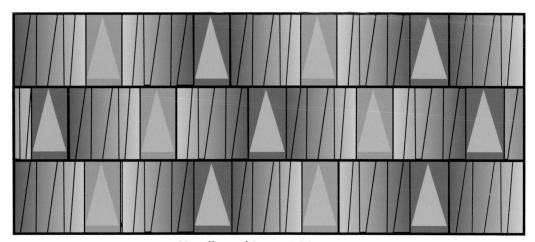

Headboard Layout Diagram

Window Valance

Finished size: 8" x 76"
Made by: Mavis Rosbach

Materials

See the robin, towhee, goldfinch, kingfisher, blue jay and chickadee bird blocks on pages 112, 118, 131, 137, 140 and 146 for fabric requirements, or select different birds of choice.

» ⅓-yard green batik fabric (binding and tabs)

» ¾-yard total of assorted green fabrics (tree blocks)

» ¼-yard blue batik fabric (tree blocks)

» 2" scraps brown fabrics* (tree blocks)

» ½-yard green print fabric (backing)

» Lightweight batting

» Tree Piecing Pattern (page 103)

*The number of scraps needed for the tree trunks will depend on the number of blocks needed to custom-fit your window.

Cutting Plan

From the green batik fabric, cut:
  • four 2½" x 42" strips for the binding and tabs
From the green print fabric, cut:
  • one 8½" x 76½" backing piece

»»Set the stage for viewing your back yard with a paper-pieced valance!««

Instructions

Note: All seam allowances are ¼" unless otherwise instructed.

Assemble the Valance Top

Refer to the layout diagram on the next page, if necessary, while assembling the window valance.

1. Paper-piece six bird blocks, following the instructions on pages 9 through 13, 112, 118, 131, 137, 140 and 146.

2. Paper-piece seven tree blocks, following the instructions on pages 9 through 13 and 103.

3. Arrange the bird and tree blocks as they will appear in the finished valance, following the Valance Layout Diagram on the next page.

4. Stitch the blocks into a row.

5. Remove the paper.

6. Press the seam allowances in one direction.

Step 2

Step 1: Just as with many of the projects in this book, you can either vary the bird blocks in valance, as shown here, use just one type of bird block, or try different combinations.

Make the Hanging Tabs

1. Stitch the long edges of two 2½" strips together (Figure 5-17).

2. Turn right-side out and press.

3. Cut the strips into 5½ lengths; need 13 (Figure 5-18).

4. Fold each 5½" length in half and pin to the top edge of the valance, centering one on the top of each block (Figure 5-19).

5. Baste in place.

Finish the Valance

Layer, quilt and bind the valance, following the instructions on pages 16 through 18, catching the hanging tabs in the binding as you sew.

Figure 5-17   Figure 5-18

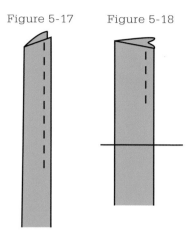

Figure 5-19

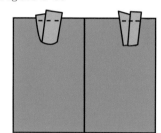

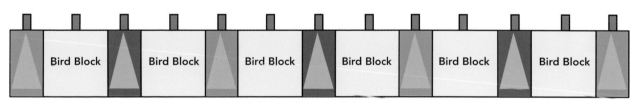

| Bird Block | Bird Block | Bird Block | Bird Block | Bird Block | Bird Block |

Valance Layout Diagram

Robin

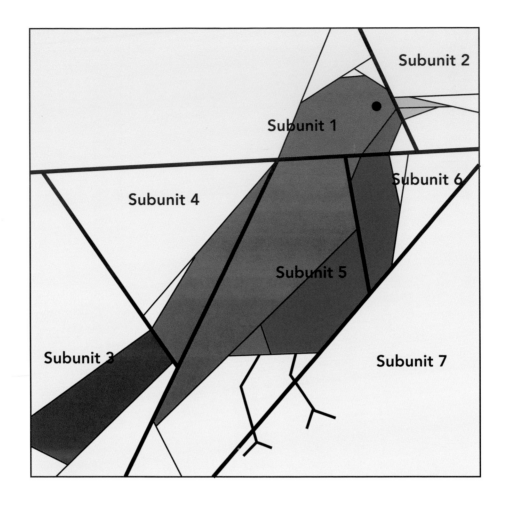

Robin Piecing Pattern » » » » » Finished size: 8" square

Fabric Requirements*

- 7" x 8" piece brown fabric (back, head and wing)
- 4" x 3" piece dark brown fabric (tail)
- 4" x 5" piece red fabric (breast)
- 2" square yellow fabric (beak)
- 2" square rust fabric (throat and under wing)
- 7" x 18" piece blue fabric (background)

*Fabric requirements are estimates. Due to the paper-piecing method, you may use more or less.

Piecing Instructions

Subunit piecing order; sew as follows:
Subunit 1 to 2
Subunit 3 to 4
Subunits 5 to 6
Subunits 3-4 to 5-6
Subunits 3-4-5-6 to 7
Subunits 1-2 to 3-4-5-6-7

Robin

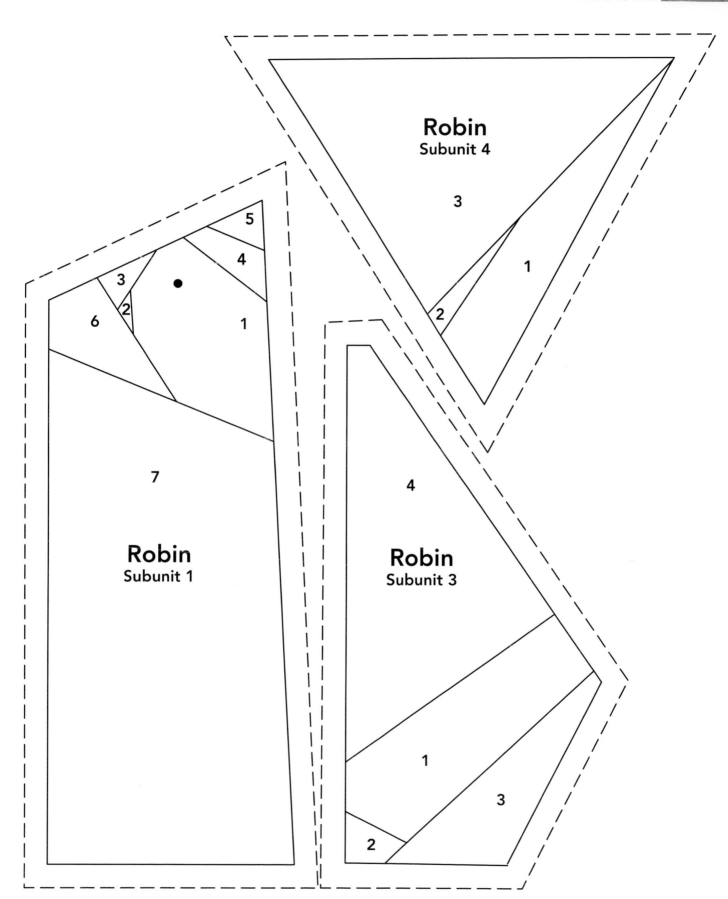

Robin
Subunit 4

3

1

2

Robin
Subunit 1

5
4
3
2
1
6
7

Robin
Subunit 3

4

1
3
2

Robin

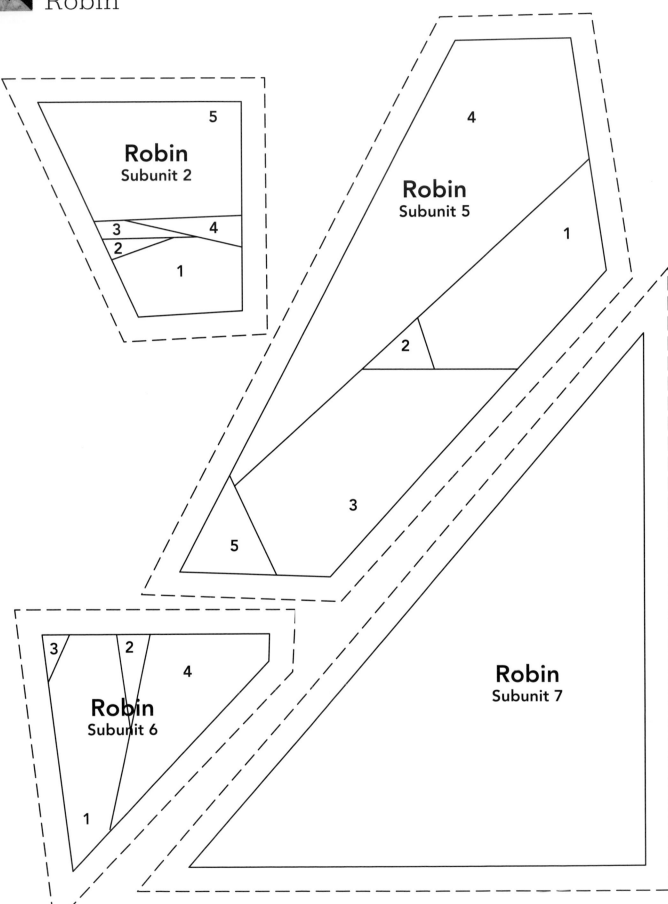

Robin
Subunit 2

5

3 4

2

1

Robin
Subunit 5

4

1

2

3

5

Robin
Subunit 6

3 2

4

1

Robin
Subunit 7

Cardinal

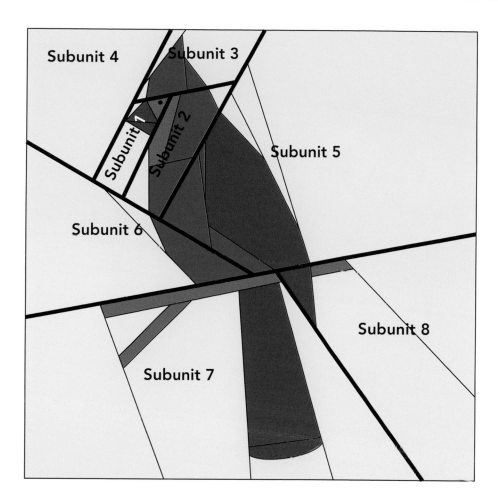

Subunit 4   Subunit 3

Subunit 1

Subunit 2

Subunit 5

Subunit 6

Subunit 7

Subunit 8

Cardinal Piecing Pattern » » » » » Finished size: 8" square

Fabric Requirements*

- 4" x 8" piece red #1 fabric (wing and tail)
- 4" x 8" piece red #2 fabric (head, neck and breast)
- 3" square gray fabric (face)
- 2" square black fabric (beak)
- 4" x 6" piece brown fabric (tree branch)
- 8" x 18" piece blue fabric (background)

*Fabric requirements are estimates. Due to the paper-piecing method, you may use more or less.

Piecing Instructions

Subunit piecing order; sew as follows:
Subunit 1 to 2
Subunit 3 to 1-2
Subunit 4 to 1-2-3
Subunit 5 to 1-2-3-4
Subunit 6 to 1-2-3-4-5
Subunit 7 to 8
Subunit 7-8 to 1-2-3-4-5-6

Cardinal

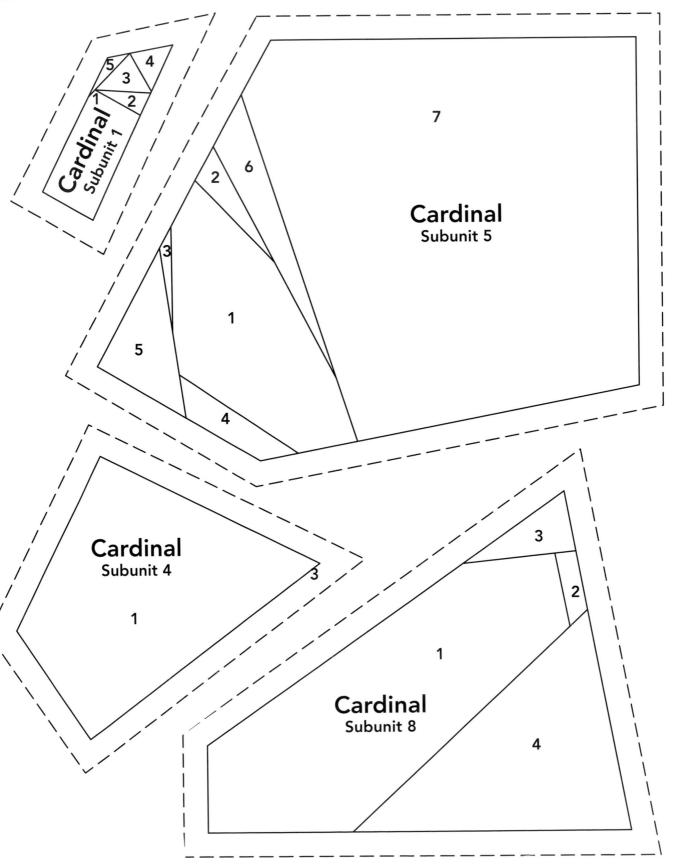

Cardinal
Subunit 1

5 4
3
1 2

2 6

3

1

5

4

7

Cardinal
Subunit 5

Cardinal
Subunit 4

3

1

3

2

1

Cardinal
Subunit 8

4

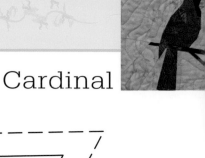

Cardinal

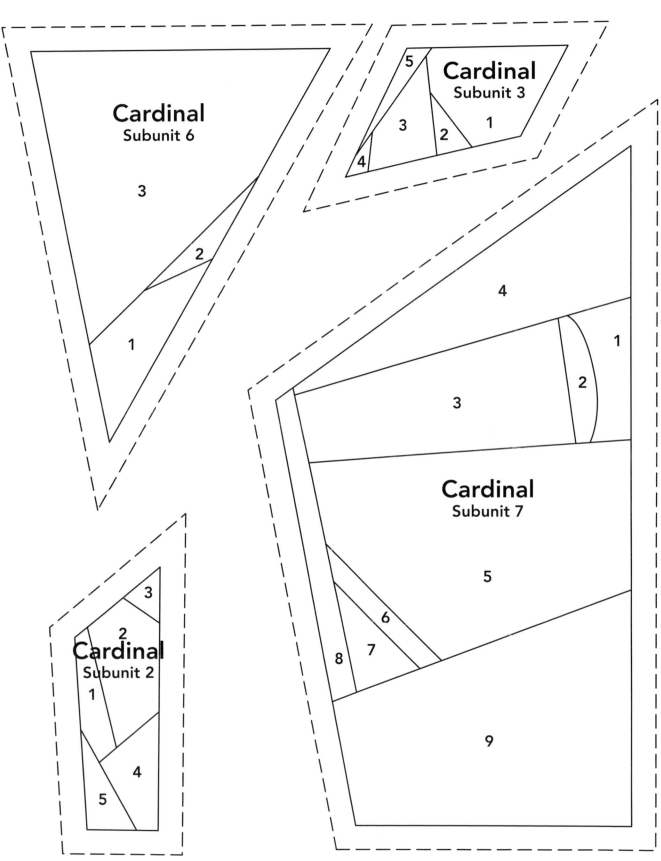

Cardinal
Subunit 6

3

2

1

Cardinal
Subunit 3

5
3
2
1
4

Cardinal
Subunit 7

4

3

1

2

5

6

7

8

9

Cardinal
Subunit 2

3

2

1

4

5

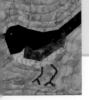

Towhee

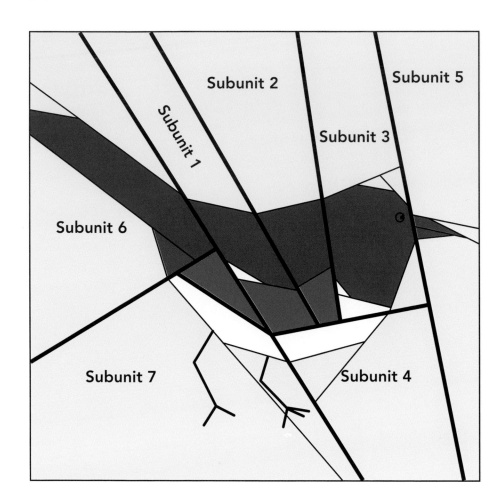

Towhee Piecing Pattern » » » » Finished size: 8" square

Fabric Requirements*

- 5" x 11" piece black fabric (head, back and tail)
- 3" x 6" piece rust fabric (wing)
- 2" x 4" piece brown fabric (beak and under tail)
- 4" x 8" piece white fabric (breast/belly)
- 6" x 18" piece blue fabric (background)

*Fabric requirements are estimates. Due to the paper-piecing method, you may use more or less.

Piecing Instructions

Subunit piecing order; sew as follows:
Subunit 1 to 2
Subunit 3 to 1-2
Subunit 4 to 1-2-3
Subunit 5 to 1-2-3-4
Subunit 6 to 7
Subunit 6-7 to 1-2-3-4-5

Towhee

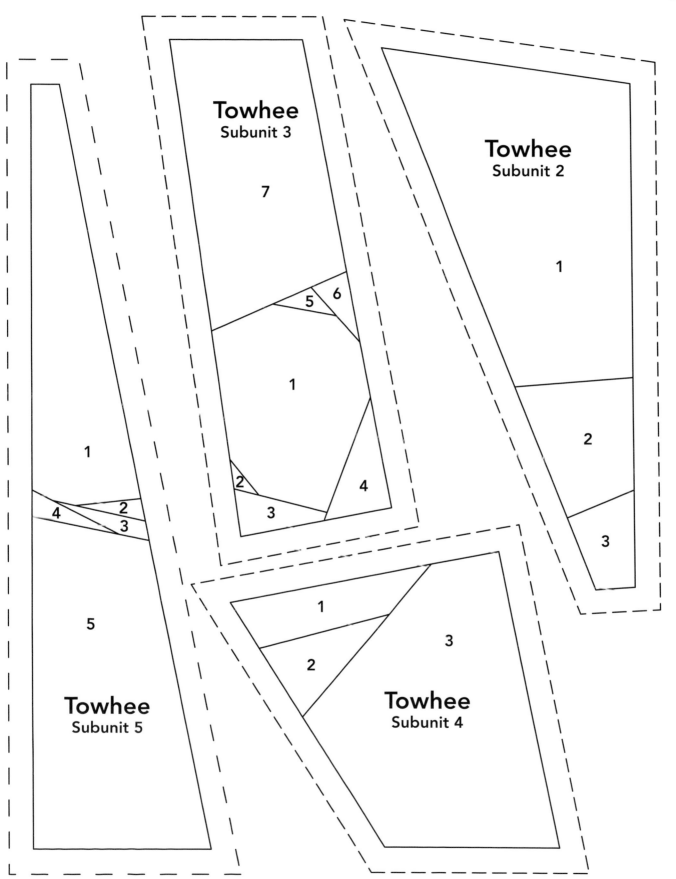

Towhee
Subunit 3

7

5   6

1

2

3

4

Towhee
Subunit 2

1

2

3

1

4

2

3

5

1

2

3

Towhee
Subunit 5

Towhee
Subunit 4

Towhee

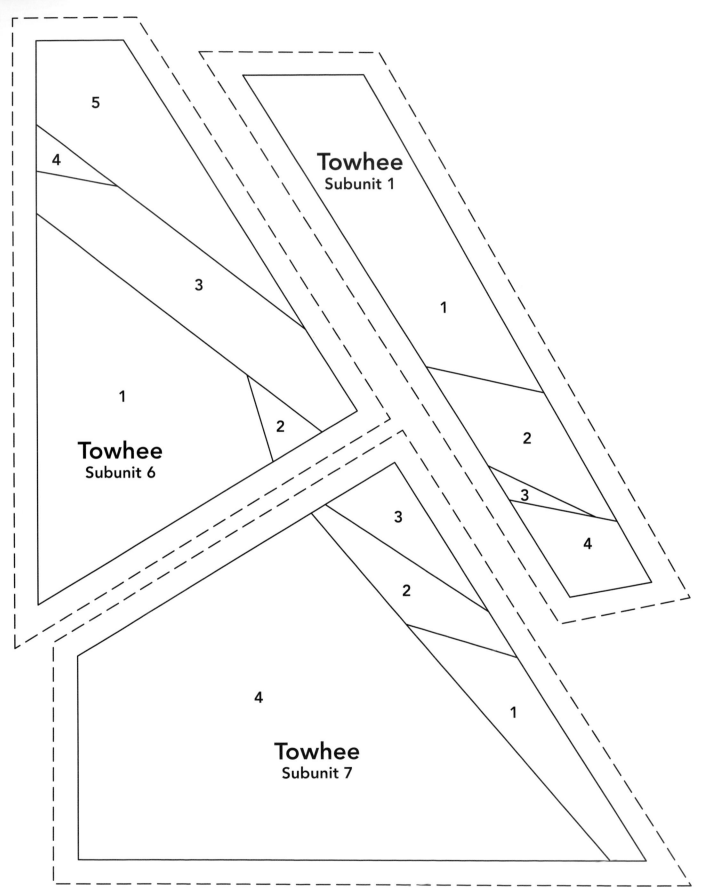

Towhee Subunit 1

Towhee Subunit 6

Towhee Subunit 7

Wren

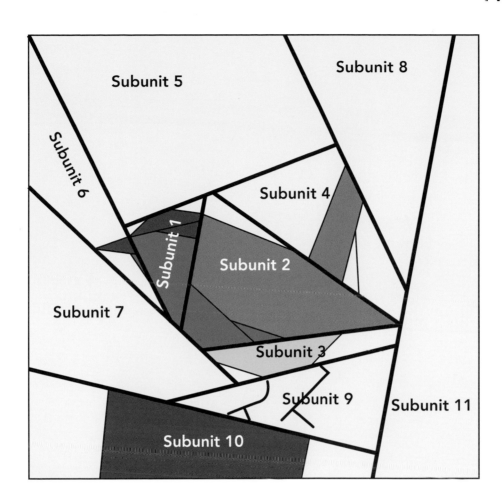

Wren Piecing Pattern » » » » »

Finished size: 8" square

Fabric Requirements*

- 3" x 2" piece dark brown fabric (head)
- 5" x 6" piece medium brown fabric (wing and tail)
- 4" x 6" piece light brown fabric (throat and breast)
- 4½" x 3" piece brown #4 fabric (stump)
- 2" square black fabric (beak)
- 3½" x 2" piece beige fabric (belly)
- 9" x 16" piece blue fabric (background)

*Fabric requirements are estimates. Due to the paper-piecing method, you may use more or less.

Piecing Instructions

Subunit piecing order; sew as follows:
Subunit 1 to 2
Subunit 3 to 1-2
Subunit 4 to 1-2-3
Subunit 5 to 1-2-3-4
Subunit 6 to 1-2-3-4-5
Subunit 7 to 1-2-3-4-5-6
Subunit 8 to 1-2-3-4-5-6-7
Subunit 9 to 1-2-3-4-5-6-7-8
Subunit 10 to 1-2-3-4-5-6-7-8-9
Subunit 11 to 1-2-3-4-5-6-7-8-9-10

Wren

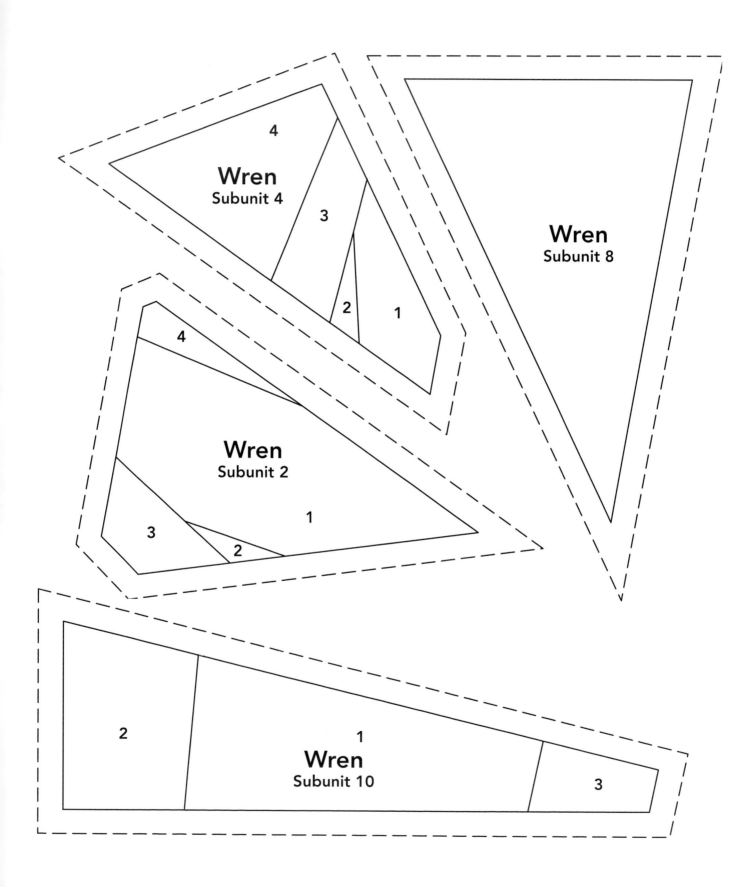

Wren
Subunit 4

4

3

2 1

Wren
Subunit 8

4

Wren
Subunit 2

1

3

2

2

1

Wren
Subunit 10

3

Wren

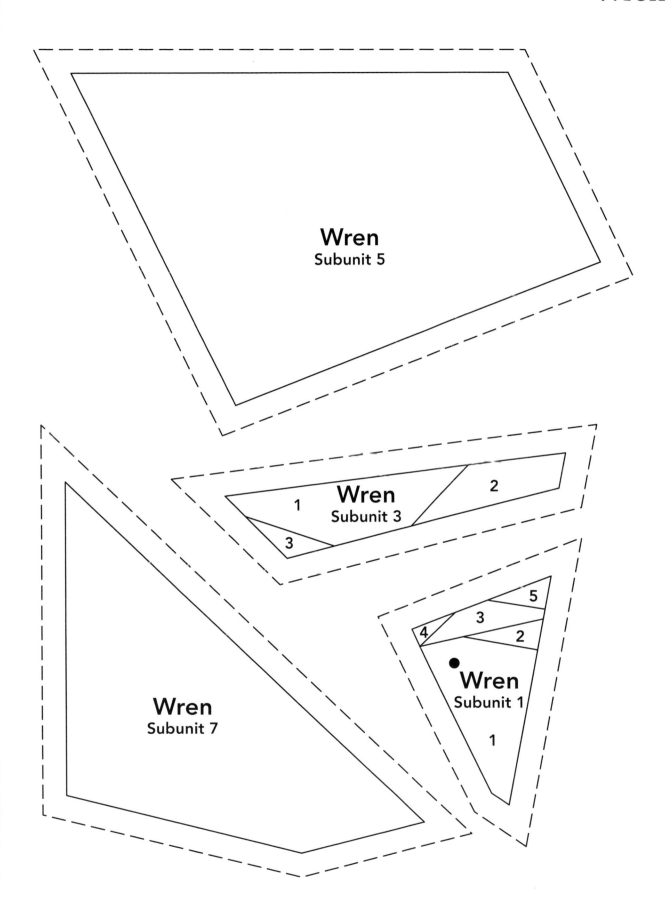

Wren
Subunit 5

Wren
Subunit 3

1

2

3

Wren
Subunit 7

5

3

4

2

Wren
Subunit 1

1

Wren

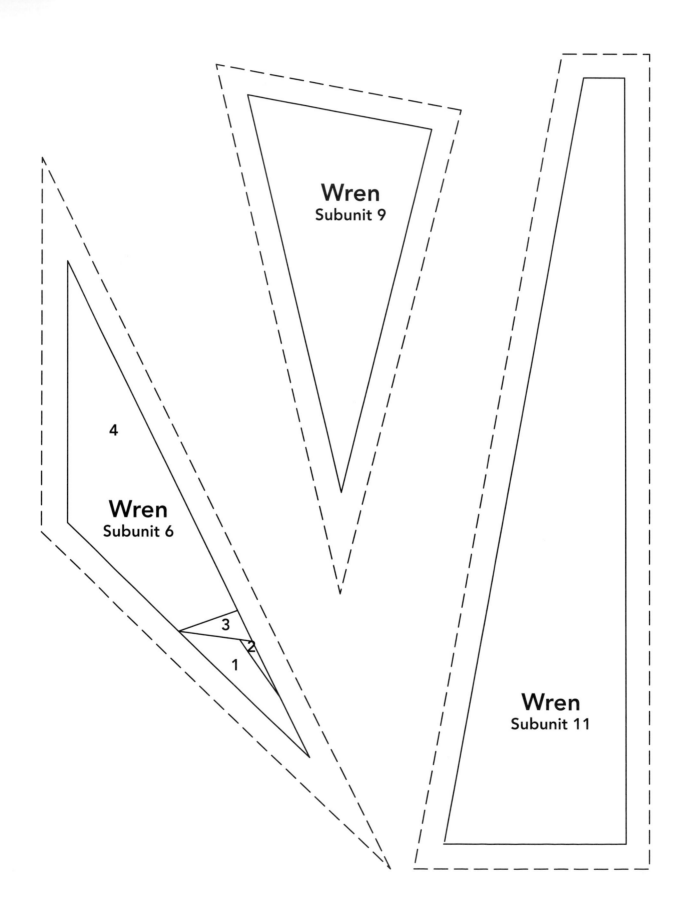

Wren
Subunit 9

4

Wren
Subunit 6

3

2

1

Wren
Subunit 11

Hummingbird

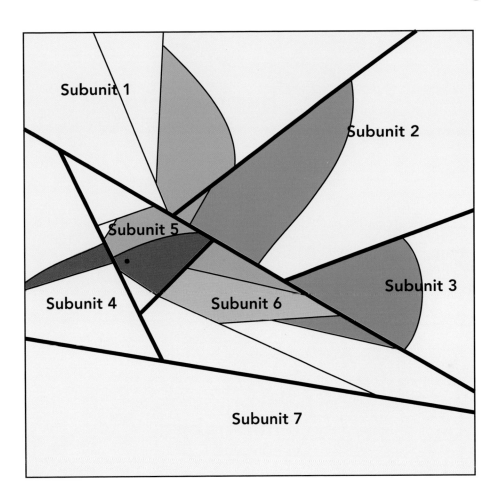

Hummingbird Piecing Pattern » » » » » Finished size: 8" square

Fabric Requirements*

- 3" x 4" piece red fabric (face/neck)
- 5" x 9" piece green fabric (head, back and back wing)
- 8" square dark green fabric (front wing and tail)
- 4" x 2" piece beige fabric (breast/belly)
- 3" x 2" piece brown fabric (beak)
- 9" x 18" piece blue fabric (background)

*Fabric requirements are estimates. Due to the paper-piecing method, you may use more or less.

Piecing Instructions

Note: To paper-piece the curves for the tail and wings, turn to page 12.

Subunit piecing order; sew as follows:
Subunit 1 to 2
Subunit 3 to 1-2
Subunit 5 to 6
Subunit 4 to 5-6
Subunit 7 to 4-5-6
Subunit 1-2-3 to 4-5-6-7

Hummingbird

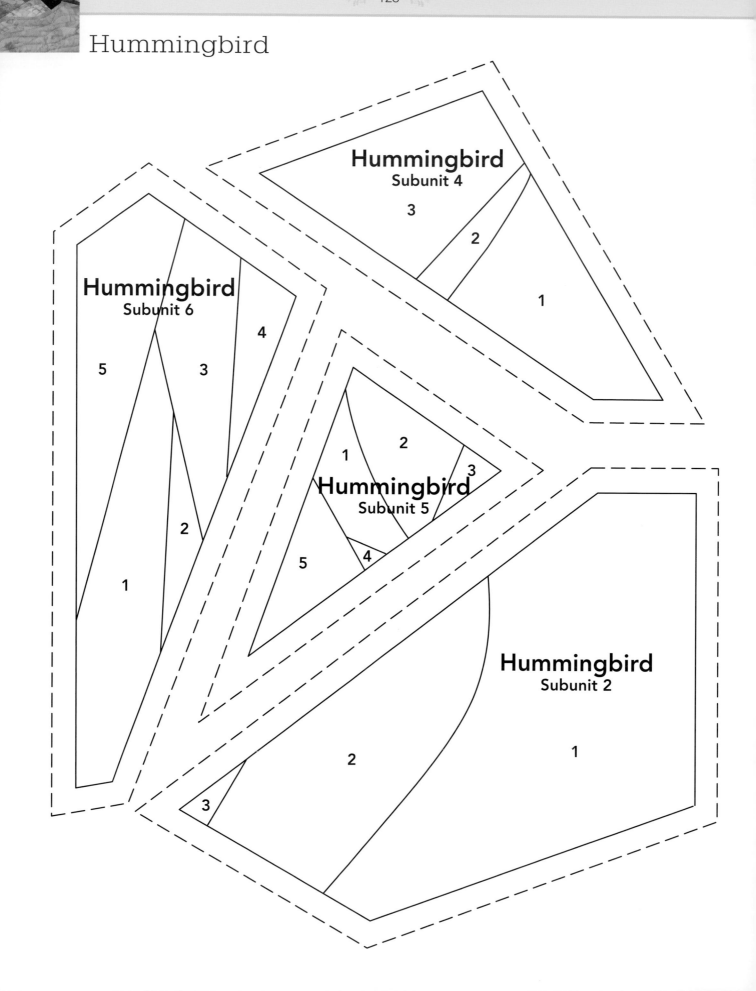

Hummingbird
Subunit 4

3

2

1

Hummingbird
Subunit 6

5

4

3

2

1

Hummingbird
Subunit 5

1

2

3

5

4

Hummingbird
Subunit 2

2

1

3

Hummingbird

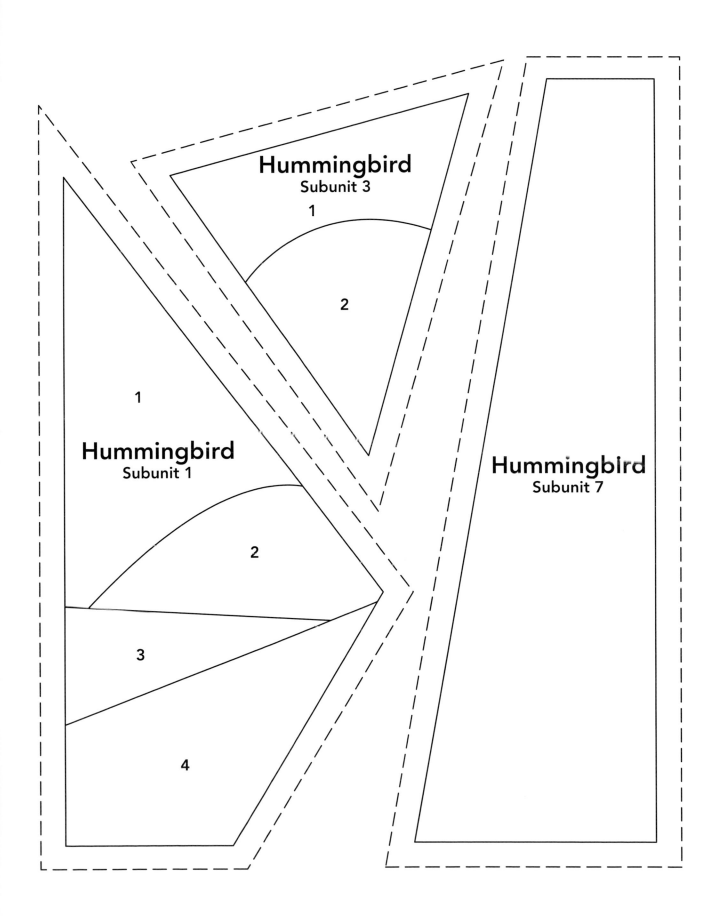

Hummingbird
Subunit 3

1

2

Hummingbird
Subunit 1

1

2

3

4

Hummingbird
Subunit 7

Bluebird

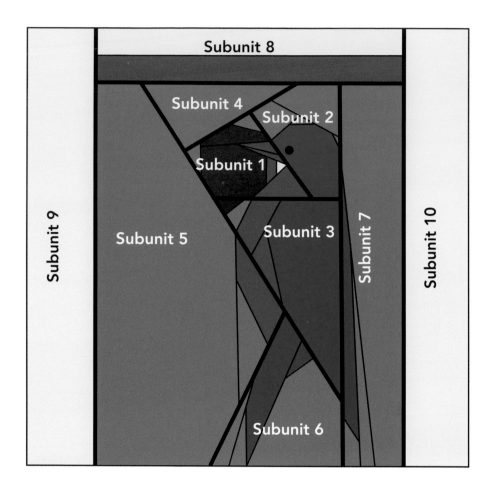

Bluebird Piecing Pattern » » » » » Finished size: 8" square

Fabric Requirements*

- 6" x 10" piece blue fabric (head, wing and tail)
- 3" x 8" piece rust fabric (throat, breast and belly)
- 2" square brown #1 fabric (beak)
- 8" x 14" piece brown #2 fabric (birdhouse)
- 1½" x 6½" piece brown #3 fabric (birdhouse roof)
- 2" x 6" piece gray fabric (birdhouse hole)
- 9" x 6" piece blue fabric (background)

*Fabric requirements are estimates. Due to the paper-piecing method, you may use more or less.

Piecing Instructions

Subunit piecing order; sew as follows:
Subunit 1 to 2
Subunit 3 to 1-2
Subunit 4 to 1-2-3
Subunit 5 to 6
Subunit 5-6 to 1-2-3-4
Subunit 7 to 1-2-3-4-5-6
Subunit 8 to 1-2-3-4-5-6-7
Subunit 9 to 1-2-3-4-5-6-7-8
Subunit 10 to 1-2-3-4-5-6-7-8-9

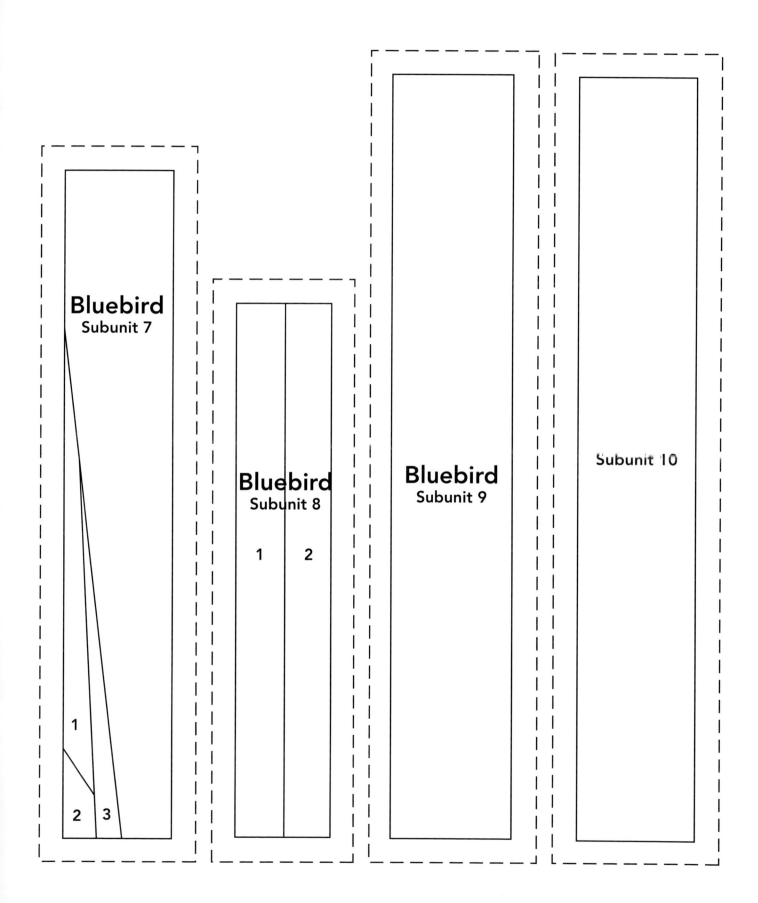

Bluebird
Subunit 7

1

2 3

Bluebird
Subunit 8

1   2

Bluebird
Subunit 9

Subunit 10

Bluebird

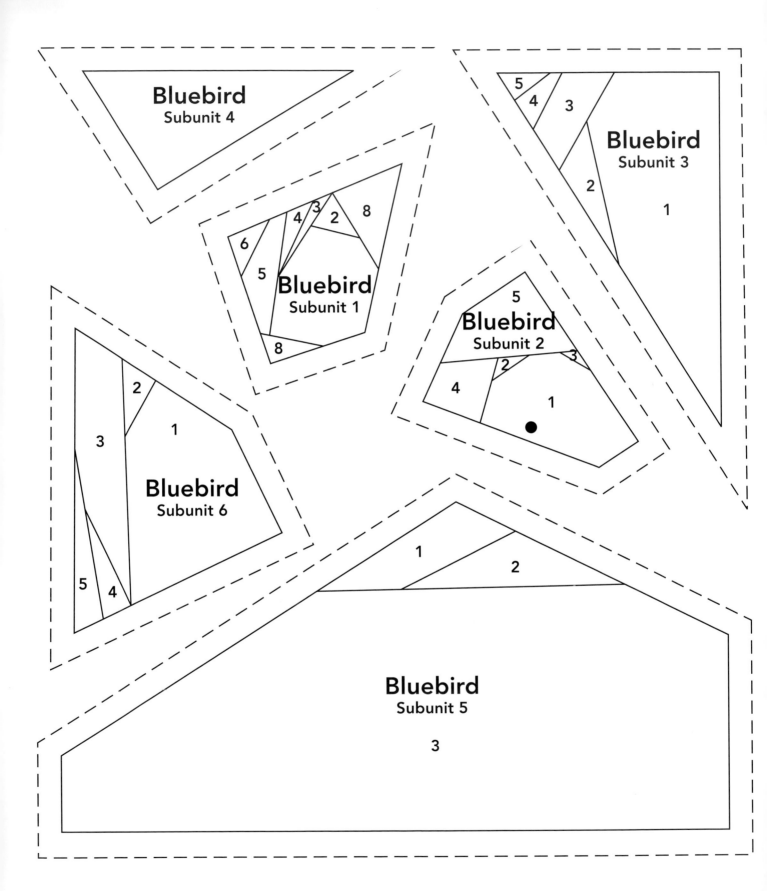

Bluebird
Subunit 4

Bluebird
Subunit 3

5
4
3
2
1

4 3 2 8
6
5
Bluebird
Subunit 1
8

5
Bluebird
Subunit 2
2 3
4
1
●

3
2
1
Bluebird
Subunit 6
5 4

1
2

Bluebird
Subunit 5

3

Goldfinch

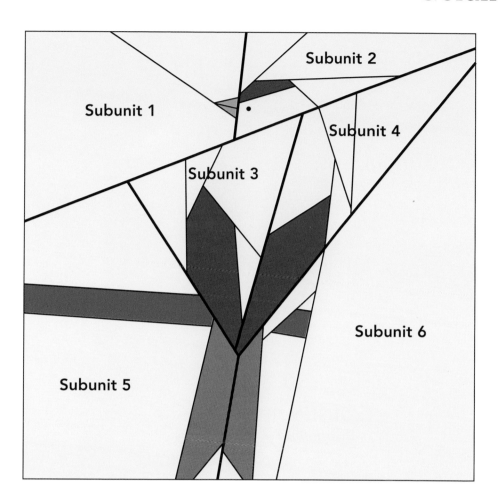

Goldfinch Piecing Pattern » » » » » Finished size: 8" square

Fabric Requirements*

- 4" x 8" piece yellow fabric (face and back/wings)
- 4" x 6" piece black fabric (wings and head)
- 4" square dark gray fabric (tail)
- 2" square gold fabric (beak)
- 4" square brown fabric (tree branch)
- 9" x 12" piece blue fabric (background)

*Fabric requirements are estimates. Due to the paper-piecing method, you may use more or less.

Piecing Instructions

Subunit piecing order; sew as follows:
Subunit 1 to 2
Subunit 3 to 4
Subunit 5 to 3-4
Subunit 6 to 3-4-5
Subunit 1-2 to 3-4-5-6

When you sew Subunit 6 to 3-4-5, you will have to sew a "set-in" seam. This is easy with the paper. Simply pin and stitch Subunit 6 to Subunit 5, following the lines on the paper. Then position the pieces, pin and stitch Subunit 6 to Subunit 4. In other words, you sew one seam, but do it in two segments. The lines on the paper make it easy.

Goldfinch

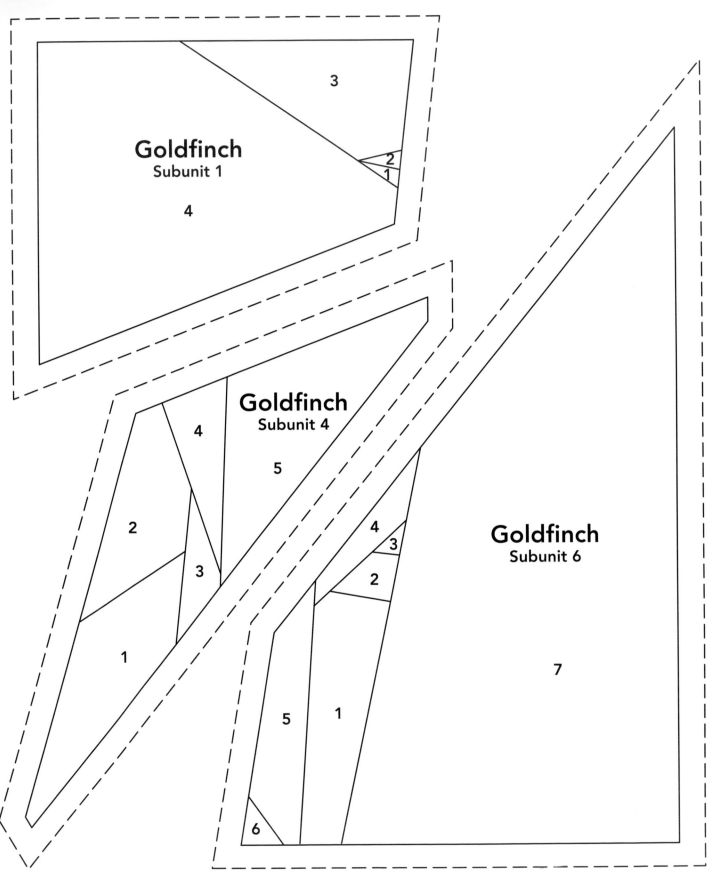

Goldfinch
Subunit 1

3

2
1

4

Goldfinch
Subunit 4

4

5

2

3

1

Goldfinch
Subunit 6

4
3
2

7

5
1

6

Goldfinch

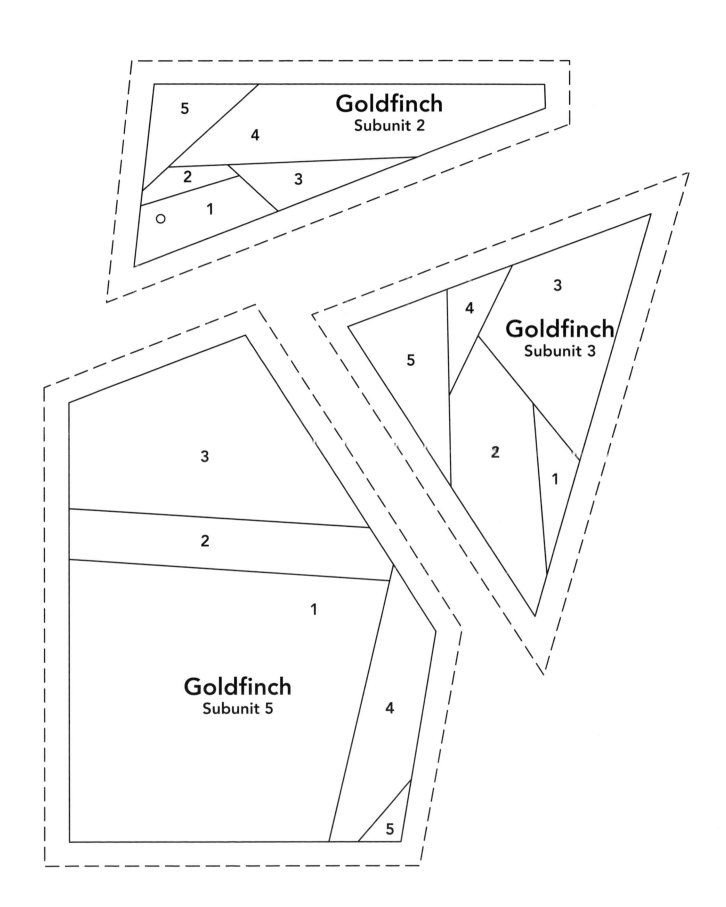

Goldfinch
Subunit 2

5

4

2

3

1

○

Goldfinch
Subunit 3

3

4

5

2

1

3

2

1

Goldfinch
Subunit 5

4

5

Canada Goose

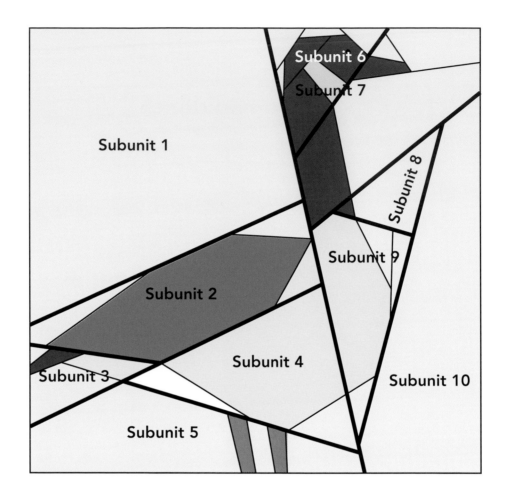

Canada Goose Piecing Pattern » » » » » Finished size: 8" square

Fabric Requirements*

- 3" x 10" piece black fabric (head, beak, neck and tail)
- 6" x 3" piece brown fabric (wing)
- 2" x 3" piece gray fabric (legs)
- 5" x 8" piece beige fabric (breast, belly and under wing)
- 4" square white fabric (throat and under wing)
- 8" x 14" piece blue fabric (background)

*Fabric requirements are estimates. Due to the paper-piecing method, you may use more or less.

Piecing Instructions

Subunit piecing order; sew as follows:
Subunit 1 to 2
Subunit 3 to 1-2
Subunit 4 to 5
Subunit 1-2-3 to 4-5
Subunit 6 to 7
Subunit 8 to 9
Subunit 10 to 8-9
Subunit 6-7 to 8-9-10
Subunit 1-2-3-4-5 to 6-7-8-9-10

Canada Goose

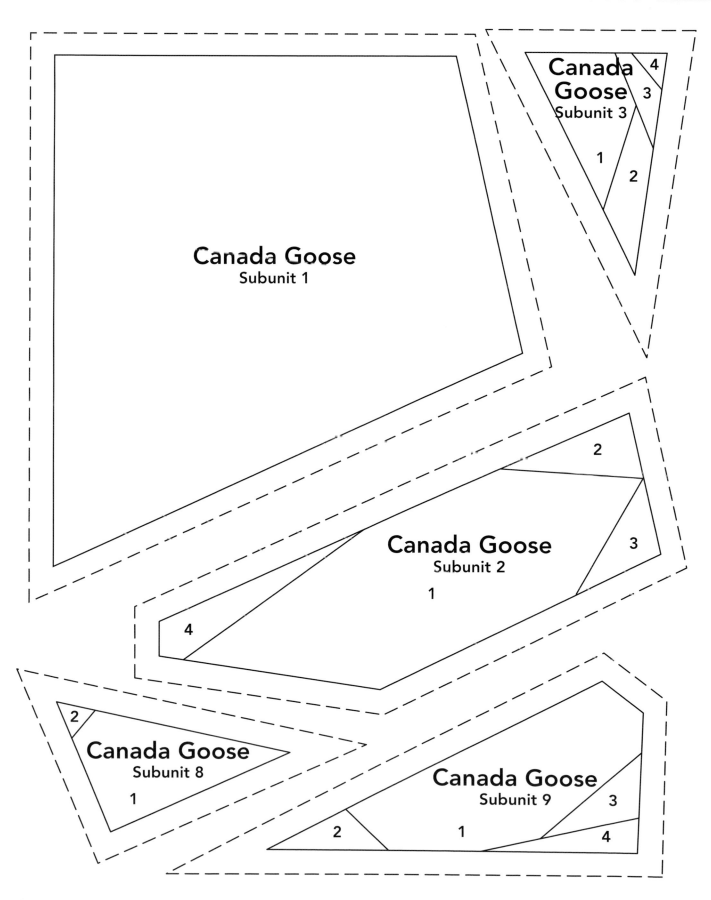

Canada Goose
Subunit 1

Canada Goose
Subunit 3

4
3
1
2

Canada Goose
Subunit 2

2
3
1
4

Canada Goose
Subunit 8

2
1

Canada Goose
Subunit 9

3
2
1
4

Canada Goose

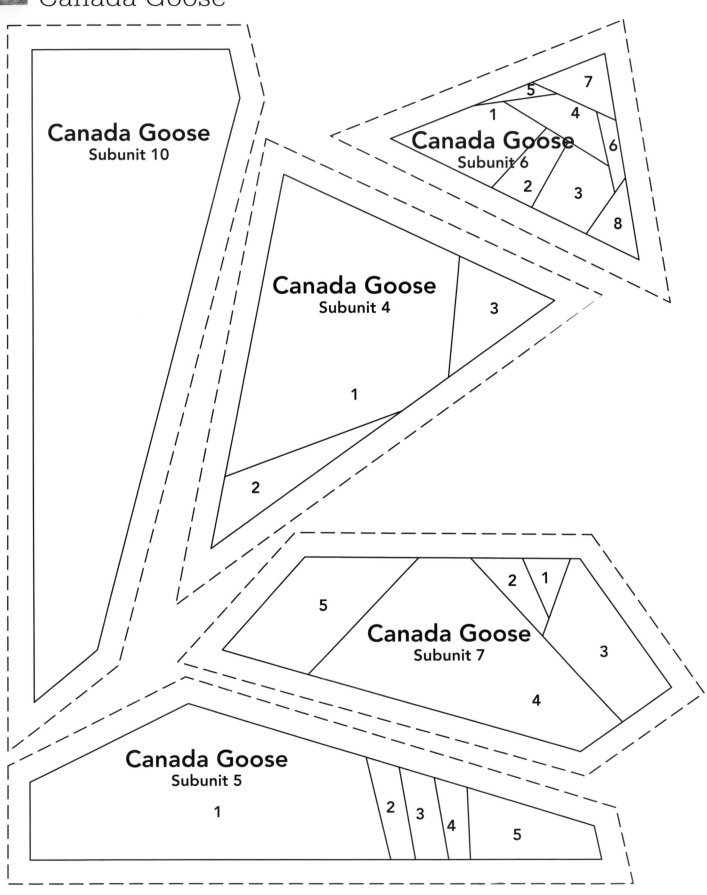

Canada Goose
Subunit 10

Canada Goose
Subunit 6

5

7

1

4

6

2

3

8

Canada Goose
Subunit 4

3

1

2

Canada Goose
Subunit 7

5

2

1

3

4

Canada Goose
Subunit 5

1

2

3

4

5

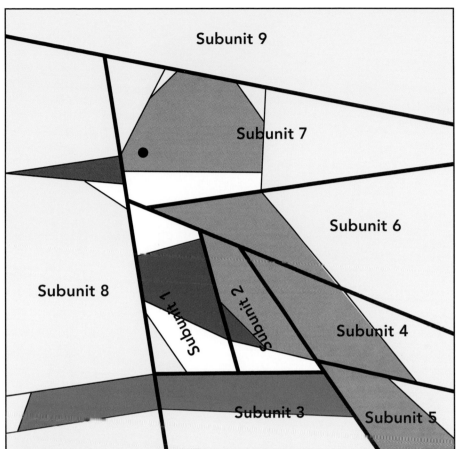

Kingfisher Piecing Pattern » »

Finished size: 8" square

Fabric Requirements*

- 4" x 10" piece light gray fabric (head, back, wing and tail)
- 3" x 2" piece dark gray fabric (upper beak)
- 4" x 7" piece white fabric (neck, lower beak, throat and belly)
- 3" x 4" piece rust fabric (breast)
- 4" square brown fabric (tree branch)
- 9" x 16" piece blue fabric (background)

*Fabric requirements are estimates. Due to the paper-piecing method, you may use more or less.

Piecing Instructions

Subunit piecing order; sew as follows:
Subunit 1 to 2
Subunit 3 to 1-2
Subunit 4 to 5
Subunit 4-5 to 1-2-3
Subunit 6 to 7
Subunit 6-7 to 1-2-3-4-5
Subunit 8 to 1-2-3-4-5-6-7
Subunit 9 to 1-2-3-4-5-6-7-8

Kingfisher

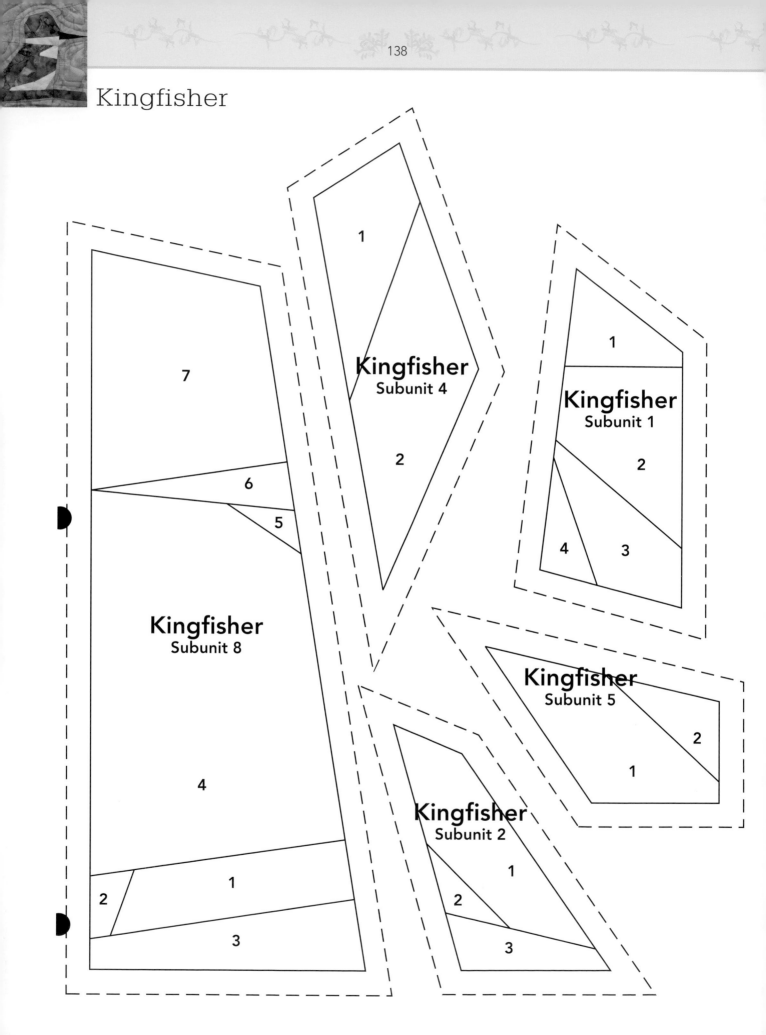

Kingfisher
Subunit 4

1

2

Kingfisher
Subunit 1

1

2

4 3

7

6

5

Kingfisher
Subunit 8

4

Kingfisher
Subunit 5

2

1

Kingfisher
Subunit 2

1

2

3

2

1

3

Kingfisher

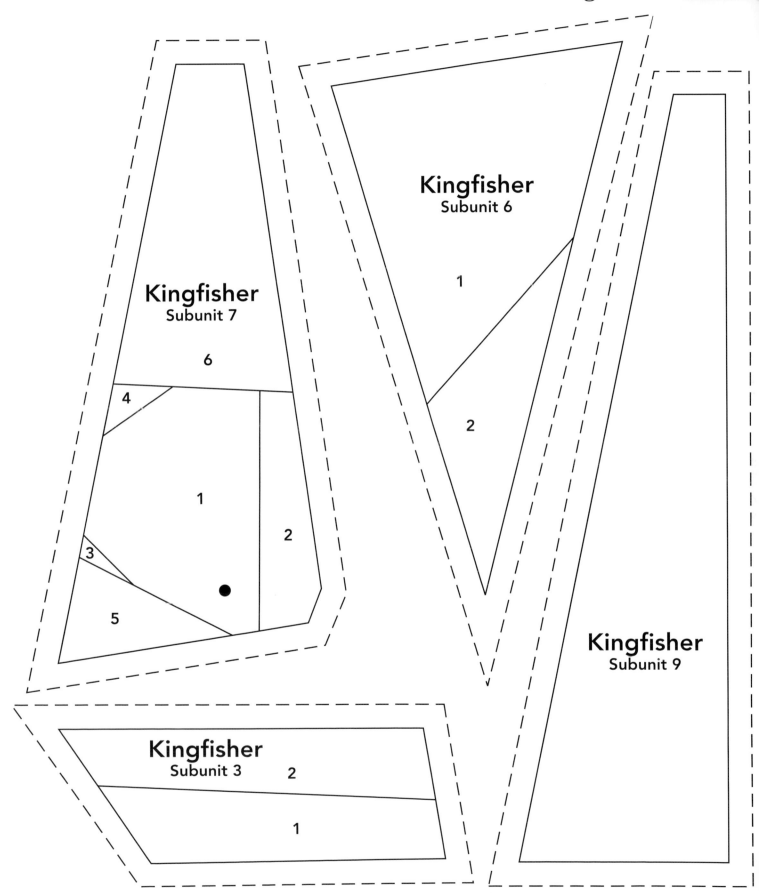

Kingfisher
Subunit 6

1

2

Kingfisher
Subunit 7

6

4

1

2

3

5

Kingfisher
Subunit 9

Kingfisher
Subunit 3

2

1

Blue Jay

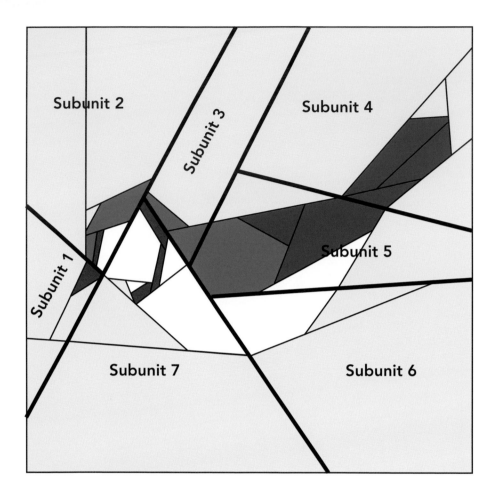

Simplified Option
(works well with batiks)

Blue Jay Piecing Pattern »»»   **Finished size:** 8" square

Fabric Requirements*

- 4" x 10" piece dark blue fabric (head, neck and partial wing)
- 4" x 6" piece medium blue fabric (partial wing and tail)
- 4" x 8" piece white fabric (partial face, partial neck, breast and belly)
- 2" x 5" piece black fabric (beak, partial face and partial neck)
- 6" x 12" piece blue fabric (background)

*Fabric requirements are estimates. Due to the paper-piecing method, you may use more or less.

Piecing Instructions

Subunit piecing order; sew as follows:
Subunit 1 to 2
Subunit 4 to 5
Subunit 6 to 4-5
Subunit 3 to 4-5-6
Subunit 7 to 3-4-5-6
Subunit 1-2 to 3-4-5-6-7

Blue Jay

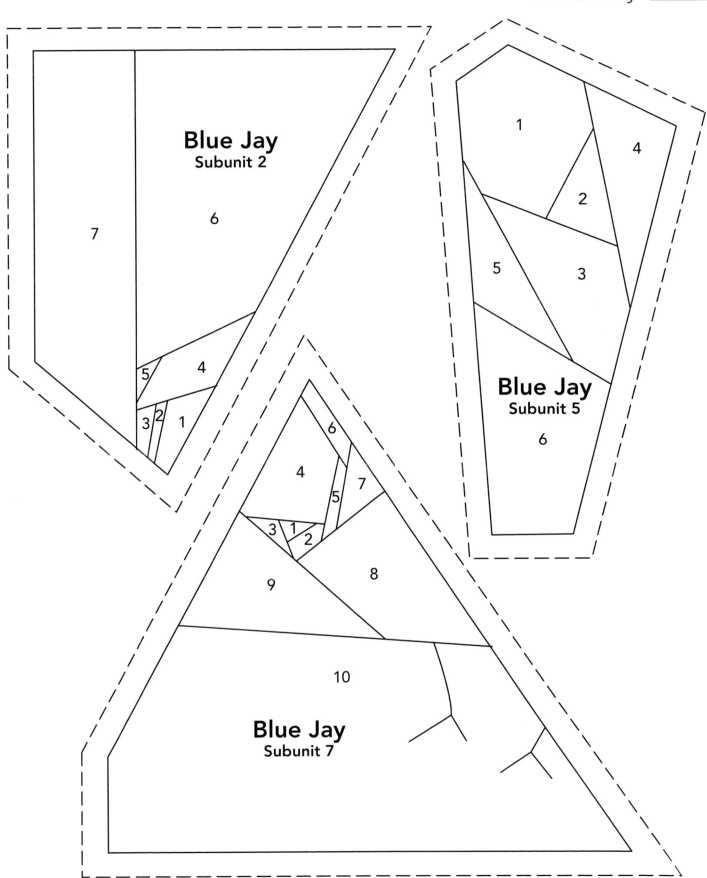

Blue Jay
Subunit 2

7

6

5

4

3 2 1

Blue Jay
Subunit 5

1

4

2

5

3

6

Blue Jay
Subunit 7

6

4

5 7

3 1 2

9

8

10

Blue Jay

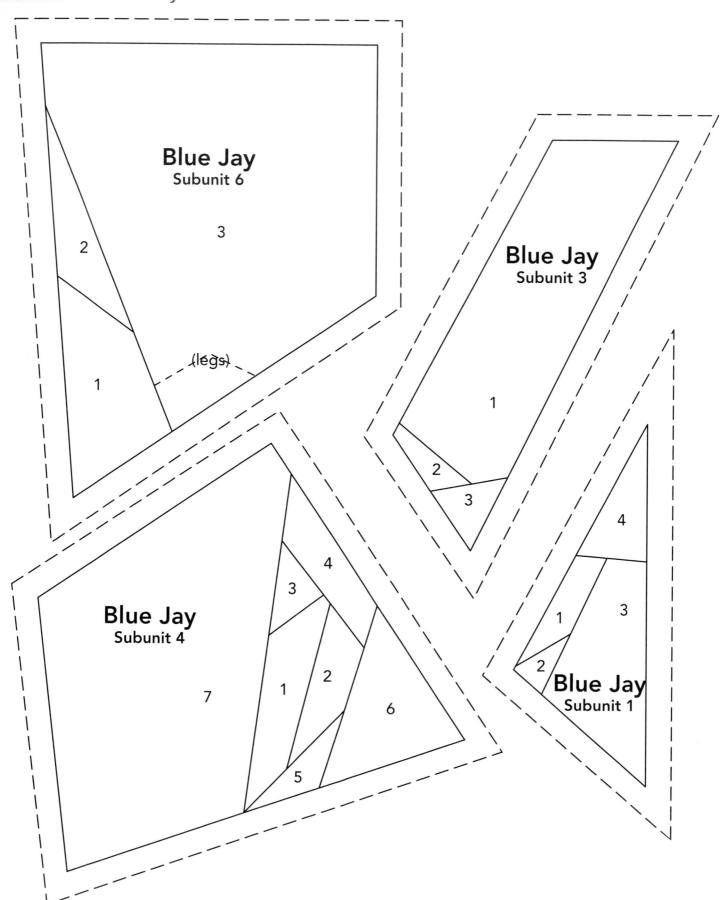

Blue Jay
Subunit 6

3

2

1

(legs)

Blue Jay
Subunit 3

1

2

3

Blue Jay
Subunit 4

3

4

1

2

7

6

5

4

1

3

2

Blue Jay
Subunit 1

Blue Jay

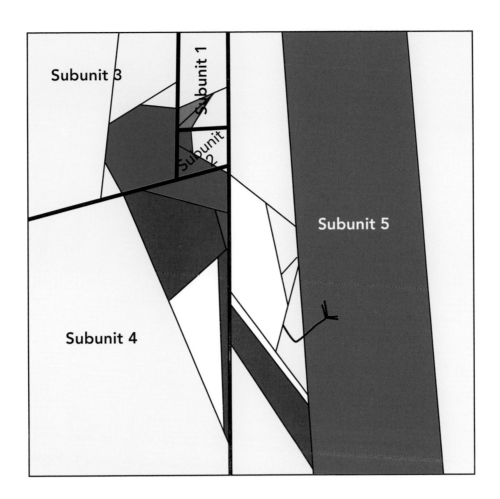

Woodpecker Piecing Pattern » Finished size: 8" square

Fabric Requirements*

- 3" x 8" piece red fabric (head and throat)
- 5" x 8" piece black fabric (partial wing and tail)
- 4" x 8" piece white fabric (partial wing and breast/belly)
- 4" x 9" piece brown fabric (tree trunk)
- 2" square dark gray fabric (beak)
- 9" x 18" piece blue fabric (background)

*Fabric requirements are estimates. Due to the paper-piecing method, you may use more or less.

Piecing Instructions

Subunit piecing order; sew as follows:
Subunit 1 to 2
Subunit 3 to 1-2
Subunit 4 to 1-2-3
Subunit 5 to 1-2-3-4

Woodpecker

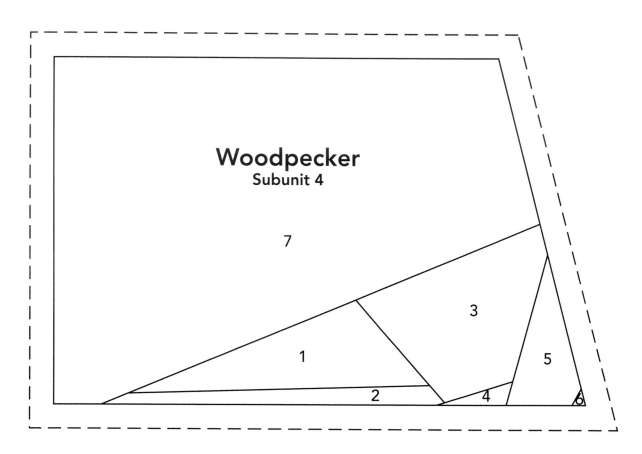

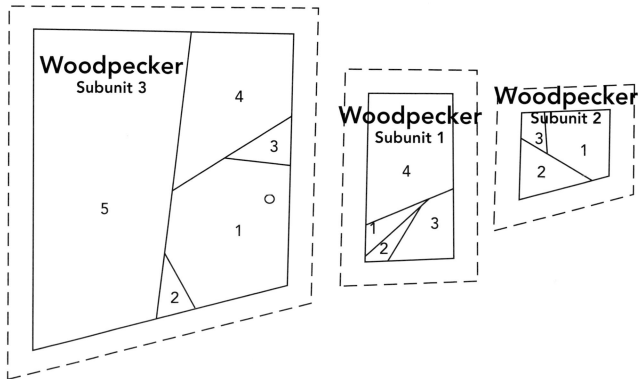

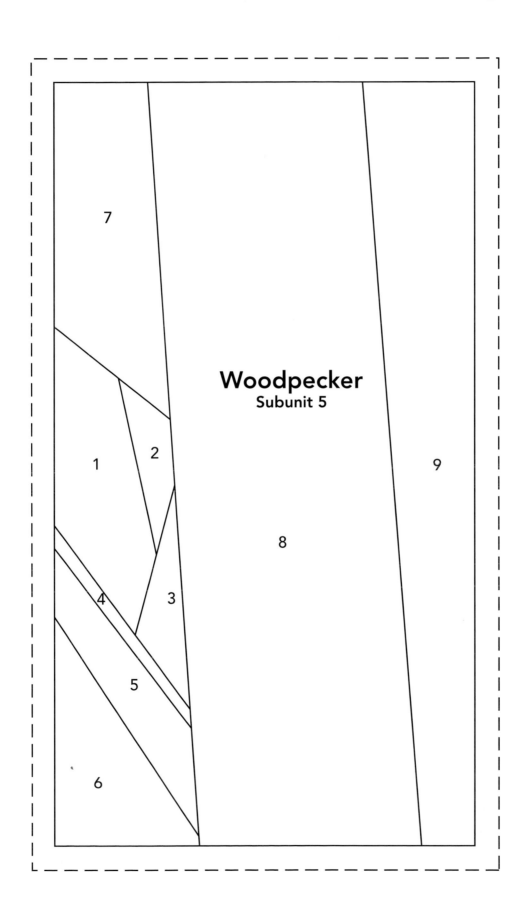

Woodpecker
Subunit 5

7

1

2

9

8

4

3

5

6

Chickadee

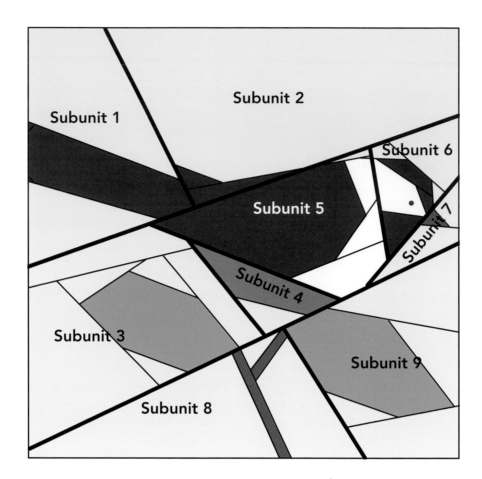

Robin Piecing Pattern » » » » » Finished size: 8" square

Fabric Requirements*

- 5" x 10" piece dark gray fabric
  (head, throat, wing, back and tail)
- 3" x 6" piece white fabric
  (face, neck and breast)
- 5" x 6" piece green fabric (leaves)
- 4" x 2" piece beige fabric (belly)
- 2" square brown fabric (beak)
- 6" x 18" piece blue fabric (background)

*Fabric requirements are estimates. Due to the paper-piecing method, you may use more or less.

Piecing Instructions

Subunit piecing order; sew as follows:
Subunit 1 to 2
Subunit 3 to 4
Subunit 5 to 3-4
Subunit 6 to 3-4-5
Subunit 7 to 3-4-5-6
Subunit 8 to 9
Subunit 1-2 to 3-4-5-6-7
Subunit 8-9 to 1-2-3-4-5-6-7

Chickadee

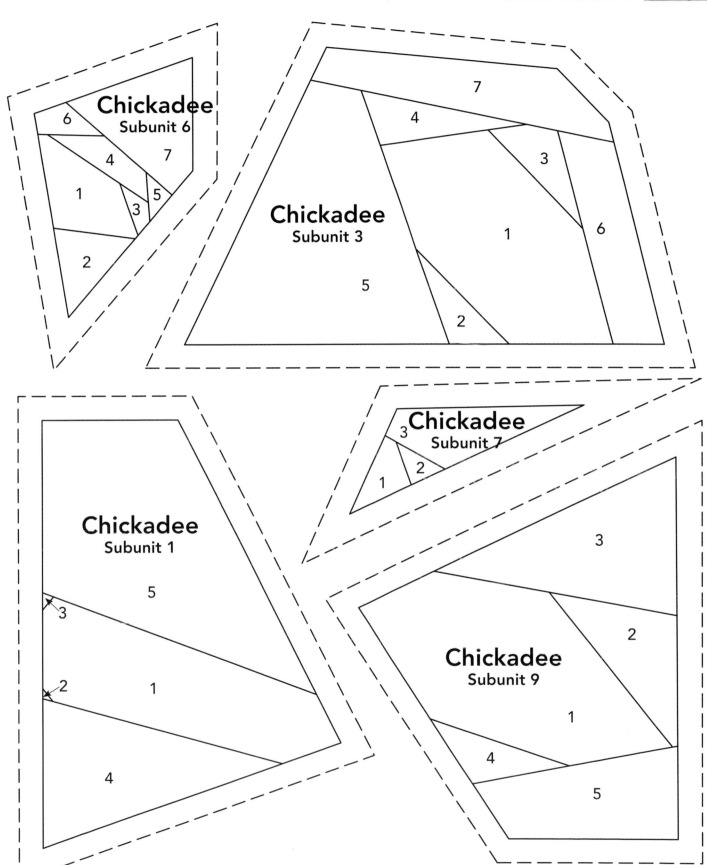

Chickadee
Subunit 6

6
4
7
1
5
3
2

Chickadee
Subunit 3

7
4
3
1
6
5
2

Chickadee
Subunit 1

5
3
2
1
4

Chickadee
Subunit 7

3
2
1

Chickadee
Subunit 9

3
2
1
4
5

Chickadee

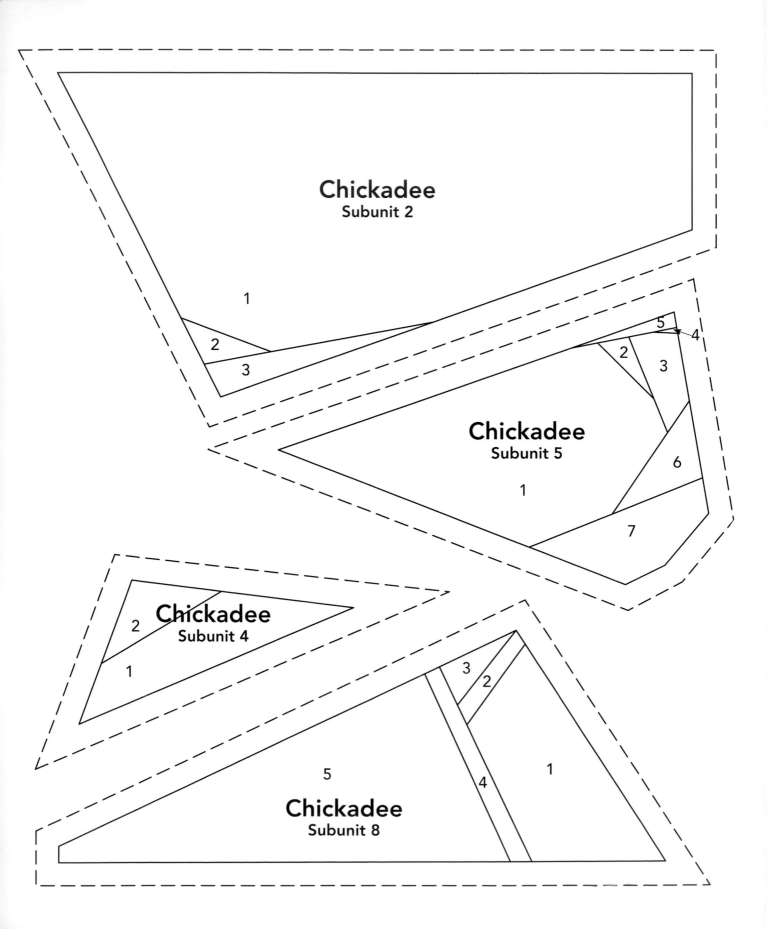

Chickadee
Subunit 2

1

2

3

5
4

2

3

Chickadee
Subunit 5

6

1

7

2

Chickadee
Subunit 4

1

3

2

5

4

1

Chickadee
Subunit 8

Simple Birds — Cardinal

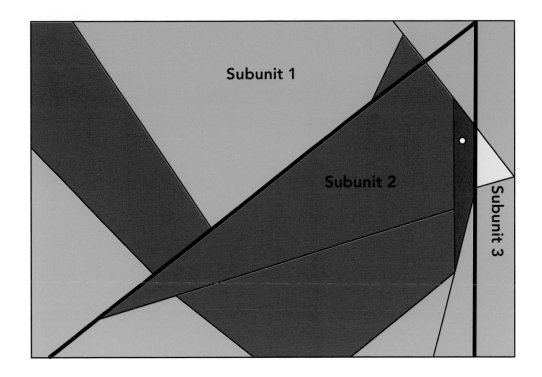

Simple Cardinal Piecing Pattern »

Finished sizes: 3½" x 5" square (small)
5½" x 8" square (large right- and left-facing)

Fabric Requirements*

- 5" x 8" piece red fabric (head, wing, breast/belly and tail)
- 2" square black fabric (face/throat)
- 2" square yellow fabric (beak)
- 4" x 8" piece green fabric (background)

*Fabric requirements are estimates. Due to the paper-piecing method, you may use more or less.

Piecing Instructions

Subunit piecing order; sew as follows:
Subunit 1 to Subunit 2.
Subunit 3 to 1-2.

Simple Birds — Small Size Cardinal

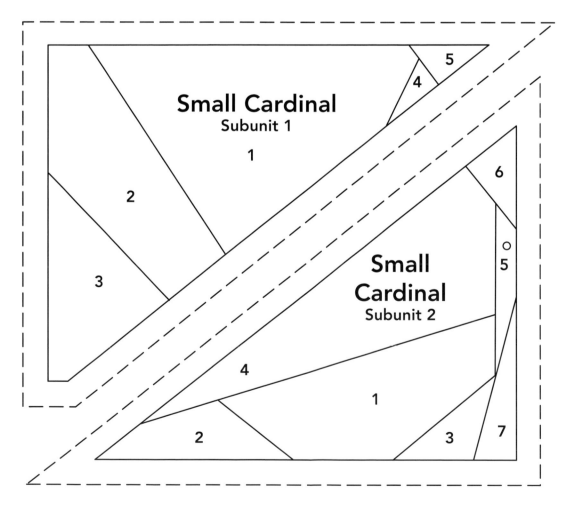

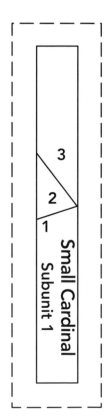

Simple Bird — Large Size Cardinal

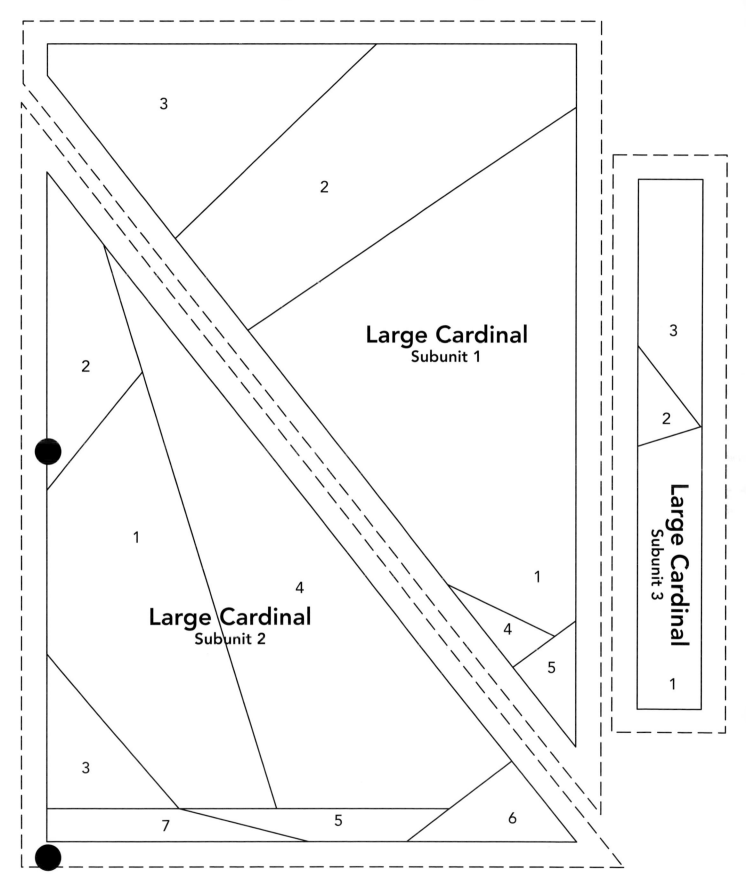

Simple Bird — Bluebird

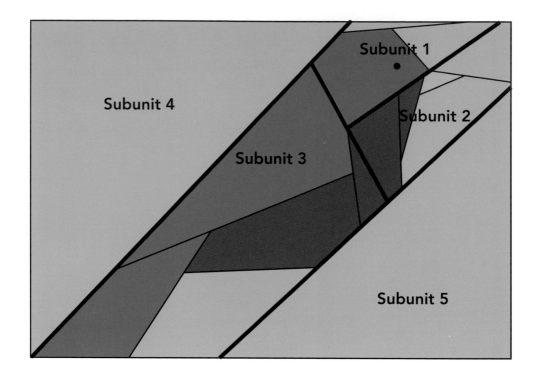

Simple Bluebird Piecing Pattern » Finished size: 3½" x 5" square (small)
5½" x 8" square (large)

Fabric Requirements*

- 4" x 6" piece blue fabric (head, wing and tail)
- 3" x 6" piece red fabic (throat, breast and belly)
- 1½" square gold fabric (beak)
- 4¼" x 7" piece green fabric (background)

*Fabric requirements are estimates. Due to the paper-piecing method, you may use more or less.

Piecing Instructions

Subunit piecing order; sew as follows:
Subunit 1 to 2.
Subunit 3 to 1-2.
Subunit 4 to 1-2-3.
Subunit 5 to 1-2-3-4.

Simple Bird — Small Size Bluebird

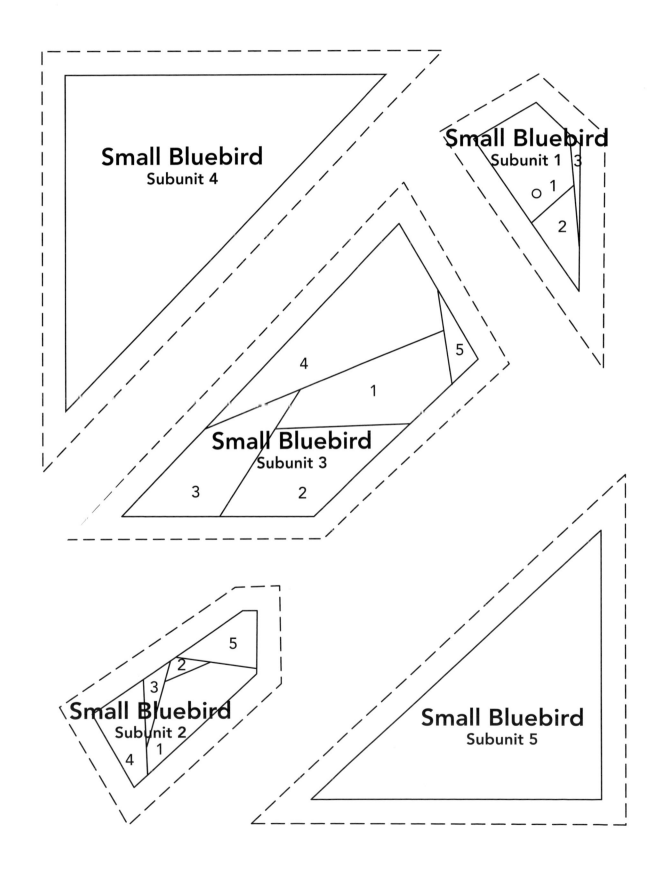

Small Bluebird
Subunit 4

Small Bluebird
Subunit 1

Small Bluebird
Subunit 3

Small Bluebird
Subunit 2

Small Bluebird
Subunit 5

Simple Bird — Large Size Bluebird

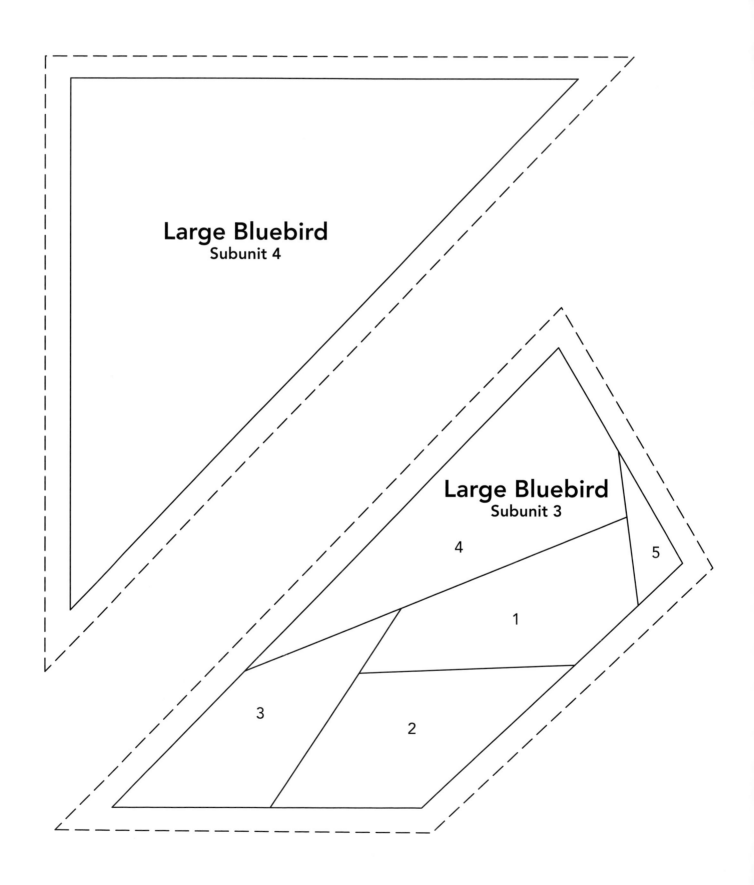

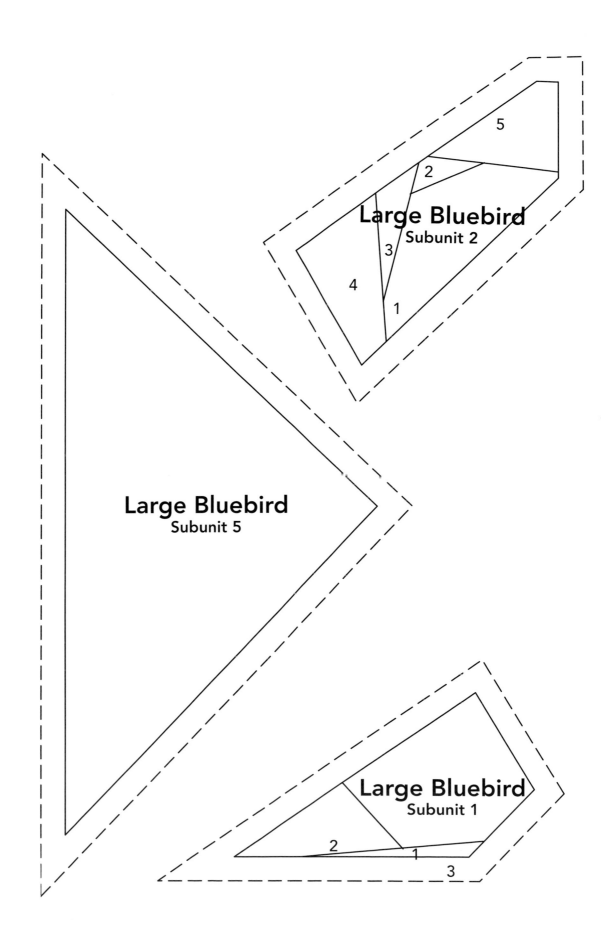

Large Bluebird
Subunit 2

5

2

3

4

1

Large Bluebird
Subunit 5

Large Bluebird
Subunit 1

2

1

3

Gallery

Once you have mastered the paper-piecing of the bird blocks in this book, the options are limitless. See what some wonderful contributors came up with and be inspired!

Do you love birds so much that you want to be around them all the time? Jayne S. Davis, the stepmother and business partner of author Jodie Davis, shows that the bird blocks are versatile enough to be incorporated into an attractive carry-along tote.

Cindy Roth of Renton, Wash., made "Christmas Cardinal" as a Christmas gift to her mother, Ruth Craig of Lake Villa, Ill. The striking look of using only the cardinal block in the center proves the old adage that "less is more!"

Floridian Laura Gamble creates a wonderful square quilt with a nine-bird design.

In "Friendship Geese," Becky Wetzel of Colchester, Vt., shows again that just one block and excellent fabric choices can come together to enhance an otherwise traditional flying geese motif.

"Birds of Summer" by Kim Calhoun of Southampton, N.J., shows exactly what it's name implies—six summer birds. The theme is further enhanced by the summertime feel of the floral borders.

Call it beginner's luck or call it just beautiful! This quilt, "A Guild of Birds," by Tina Ratermann of Silex, Mo., is her first attempt at paper-piecing. She created the quilt as her series quilt for the Pike/Lincoln Quilter's Guild 2004-05 project.

Author Jodie Davis welcomes her feathered friends—and those friends without feathers, too—year-round with these seasonal welcome signs that are easily hung outside any front door or inside the foyer. Again, these projects underline the versatility of the bird blocks, as each welcome sign is essentially constructed the same way but features different birds and fabrics to communicate a seasonal message.

"Bird Watchers Club" created by Sally Baumeister and quilted by Cindy Wilson, both of Birmingham, Ala., shows how using the bird blocks as part of a block-of-the-month Class can result in a lovely piece. Sally created this sample for the class she taught at Heart to Heart Quilt Shop in Trussville, Ala.

Joan Huckle of St. Lazare, Quebec, Canada, shows how one can create a "bird block sampler" by using 12 different bird blocks with varying backgrounds.

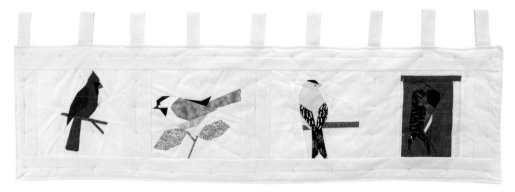

Jodie's dear friend, Christine McNeil of Greensboro, N.C., need not look out her window to enjoy her beloved birds. That's because they're on her window in this wonderful four-bird valence.

A variation of the kitchen potholder project, page 52, this potholder features a different bird block and alternate color scheme.

Amy A. Pier of Waterford, Pa., created "My Backyard," a quilt filled with birds, trees, a butterfly and even a friendly squirrel! Note that by adjusting the background piecing for each block, you too can create a cohesive outdoor scene.

"Inspiring Birds" is what Elaine Stirland of Leechburg, Pa., calls this quilt because the bird patterns kept her going while she underwent chemotherapy treatments for breast cancer. Now a survivor, Elaine says it was "as if divine guidance was helping me."

Resources

Quilting Supplies

ABC School Supply
Paper-piecing supplies
(search for "newsprint").
www.abcschoolsupply.com

American & Efird
Mettler thread
for satin stitching.
www.amefird.com
(800) 453-5128

Andover Fabrics
Gail Kessler's Manor House
(kitchen projects).
www.andoverfabrics.com
(800) 223-5678

Coats & Clark
Piecing threads and more.
www.coatsandclark.com
(800) 648-1479

Down Factory
Pillows (used in bedroom
projects), plus travel-size pillow.
www.downfactory.com
(800) 966-8700

The Electric Quilt Company
EQ Printable Foundation
Sheets and other paper-piecing
supplies.
www.electricquilt.com
(800) 356-4219

Hewlett-Packard
All-in-one printers, plus projects
devoted just to quilters.
http://h10050.www1.hp.com/
activitycenter/us/en/quilting.html
(800) 752-0900

Hobbs Bonded Fibers
Batting.
www.hobbsbondedfibers.com
(800) 433-3357

Hoffman Fabrics
Batik fabrics (bedroom projects).
www.hoffmanfabrics.com
(800) 547-0100

KP Books
Quilting books.
www.krause.com
(800) 258-0929

Mountain Mist
Heritage Collection pillow
forms.
www.starnstextiles.com
(800) 345-7150

Prym-Dritz Corp.
Collins Wash-A-Way
Foundation Paper.
www.dritz.com
(800) 845-4948

RJR Fabrics
Fabrics (porch projects).
www.rjrfabrics.com
(800) 422-5426

Sulky
Rayon threads.
www.sulky.com
(800) 874-4115

The Warm Company
Warm and Natural
Steam-A-Seam 2.
www.warmcompany.com
(800) 234-WARM (9276)

YLI
Variegated quilting threads.
www.ylicorp.com
(803) 985-3100

Birding Resources

This is a just a taste of what
the wide world of bird feeding,
watching and appreciating
has to offer. For instance,
there are sites devoted just to
hummingbirds and to purple
martins. Set off with these links
and have fun learning more
about birds.

Birder's World
Magazine.
www.birdersworld.com

Bird Watcher's Digest
Magazine.
www.birdwatchersdigest.com

**Cornell Laboratory
of Ornithology**
Project FeederWatch is just one
of the many fascinating projects
the lab runs. If you live in the
city, Project PigeonWatch may
be for you.
www.birds.cornell.edu

Droll Yankees
Seed Saver dome feeder.
www.drollyankees.com

eBird
A joint project with the Cornell
Laboratory of ornithology
and Audubon, eBird is, in its
simplest form, a way to keep
track of the birds you see. But
the power of eBird comes with
the number of observations
nationwide and the fact that
they are recorded in one place.
www.ebird.org

**The Great Back Yard
Bird Count**
Another Citizen Science project,
The Great Back Yard Bird Count
lasts just one day, providing
a picture of which species are
where at a point in time.
www.birdsource.org/gbbc

 **Project
FeederWatch**

To join and participate in this
rewarding project, visit the Web
site and also check out the
version for classrooms.
www.birds.cornell.edu/pfw

Rainbow Mealworms
Mealworms to feed birds; ships
second-day.
(800) 777-9676

Thayer's Birding Software
Software including an
encyclopedia of birds with
pictures, habitat, summer and
winter territories, etc., plus
downloadable bird songs.
www.thayerbirding.com

Other

**Furniture & Appliance Mart
Superstore**
3349 Church St.
Stevens Point, WI 54481
Name-brand furniture,
appliances, electronics and
bedding.
www.furnitureappliancemart.com
(715) 344-7700

About the Author

A passionate quilter since high school, Jodie has a knack for
stitching her interests together. This, her thirty-somethingth
book, is a case-in-point. Jodie started watching birds in her early
teens, having discovered a great horned owl nest one evening
while on horseback. She made regular visits to the nest site
thereafter to witness the progress of the chicks. She was hooked
on birds! So, of course, they must show up in her quilts.
Jodie is co-creator and host of Friends in the Bee, plus the
face you see most often on Quilter's News Network (www.
quiltersnewsnetwork.com), as she hosts three shows on the
worldwide quilting bee.